# THE PILANI PIONEERS

AF655909

# THE PILANI PIONEERS

Inspiring Success Stories of

25 BITS Pilani Graduates

GAURAV MANDLECHA
DURJAI SETHI

PAN

First published 2021 by Pan
an imprint of Pan Macmillan Publishing India Private Limited
707 Kailash Building
26 K. G. Marg, New Delhi 110 001
www.panmacmillan.co.in

Pan Macmillan, The Smithson, 6 Briset St, Farringdon, London EC1M 5NR
Associated companies throughout the world
www.panmacmillan.com

ISBN 978-81-949707-0-5

Copyright © Gaurav Mandlecha and Durjai Sethi 2021

All rights reserved. No part of this publication may be reproduced, stored in or introduced into a retrieval system, or transmitted, in any form, or by any means (electronic, mechanical, photocopying, recording or otherwise) without the prior written permission of the publisher. Any person who does any unauthorized act in relation to this publication may be liable to criminal prosecution and civil claims for damages.

3 5 7 9 8 6 4 2

This book is sold subject to the condition that it shall not, by way of trade or otherwise, be lent, re-sold, hired out, or otherwise circulated without the publisher's prior consent in any form of binding or cover other than that in which it is published and without a similar condition including this condition being imposed on the subsequent purchaser.

Typeset in Electra LT Std by R. Ajith Kumar, New Delhi
Printed and bound in India by
Replika Press Pvt. Ltd.

*To our parents for their unconditional support,*
*and to BITS Pilani, where we first attempted to understand life*

# CONTENTS

# FOREWORD

IT'S BEEN MORE THAN HALF A CENTURY SINCE I GRADUATED from BITS Pilani in 1967, but even now, I often find myself fondly reminiscing about the five years that I spent there. I still remember Postman Mahesh, who recognized every student and staff in Pilani by name, and would shout out to them if they had received a letter that day. Pilani was strictly a vegetarian place – even getting an omelette was an ordeal, let alone any meat dish. The cosmopolitan student community in Pilani had a great influence on all of us. The memories of college life, still fresh and vivid, continue to bring me utmost joy.

I felt similar happiness when the authors of this book, Gaurav Mandlecha and Durjai Sethi, requested me to write the foreword to this delightful collection of profiles of distinguished BITSian alumni. The measure of success varies across organizations and sectors of business, which is the case with the BITS fraternity as well. The BITS Alumni Association (BITSAA) – a sixty-thousand-strong community – is closely knit by the moral fibre ingrained in us by our alma mater. The sense of community that binds us together, our collective urge to give back to the society, concern for the environment and love for our country, constitute the BITSian entrepreneurial spirit.

*The Pilani Pioneers* speaks of not only the professional milestones achieved by the twenty-five outstanding individuals featured in the book, but also recounts their personal journeys which have helped them become the inspiring leaders that they are today. The book profiles young entrepreneurs like Abhishek Humbad (co-founder of Goodera) and Sagar Yarnalkar (co-founder of DailyNinja); highly successful founders, such as Gulu Mirchandani (founder and chairman of ONIDA Electronics), Hari Menon (co-founder and CEO of BigBasket); and business titans such as Sunil Duggal (the longest-serving ex-CEO of Dabur) and Harish Bhat (brand custodian of Tata Sons).

The reader is bound to be deeply inspired, as I was, by the accounts of fierce women leaders, such as Tulsi Mirchandaney (Managing Director, Blue Dart Aviation), Nandini Chopra (Managing Director, Alvarez & Marsal Corporate Finance), Shivangi Nadkarni (co-founder and CEO, Arrka Consulting) and Sandhya Prakash (Managing Director, Beacon Energy). The book holds special value to me because of the chapter on Padma Bhushan Baba Kalyani, Chairman of Bharat Forge – a contemporary who hails from a place near my hometown.

The book narrates the stories of trailblazers who share their business philosophies, the challenges they faced and how they overcame them to accomplish all that they have. I am sure readers will find the career journeys of these consummate business leaders inspirational and will also thoroughly enjoy reading about their lives outside the office. I hope this book leaves you feeling the same passion, warmth and camaraderie that resonate across the global BITSian community.

Gaurav and Durjai have done a commendable job in putting this book together after painstakingly working on it for over three years. I wish the book great success!

**Prithviraj Chavan**
Former Chief Minister of Maharashtra
BITS Pilani, Class of 1967

# INTRODUCTION

IT WAS A COLD WINTER MORNING IN JANUARY 2018 WHEN I knocked on the door of Rana Pratap 110 – Gaurav's fourth-year hostel room. He was half-asleep, I could see, but I could not bring myself to care. I asked him to accompany me for a walk, prepared to insist on it in case he wasn't enthusiastic. I forgot it was Gaurav – he was always enthusiastic.

We had walked for a few minutes, and I could sense Gaurav searching my face for an agenda. I had none; I just wanted company. For some reason, I was feeling particularly purposeless that day. I don't remember why I felt that way, but I certainly forgot about it when Gaurav started sharing the details of his rendezvous over the past year with some of the business titans he admired the most. By 'rendezvous', he meant his several unsuccessful attempts to meet these titans. As he rattled off names alien to me and explained why they were special, I interrupted him to ask how he had selected this league of extraordinary tycoons. 'They're all BITSians,' he replied as his lips curled into a smile.

Sensing my growing intrigue, he pitched the idea for the BITS Leadership Summit (BLS) – a conference through which he, and a few of my seniors, wanted to inspire peers from our college and beyond, by inviting these passionate businesspeople to talk about where they had started from, where they were now, and everything in between. BLS was truly a passion project, a venture that I, along with a few fellow BITSians, would contribute to, over the semester. Alas, it never saw the light of day, and it was our practice school's six-month-long internships due to start in July that would help us move on from the ashes of BLS.

More than a year since we buried BLS, graduated from BITS and were catapulted into the corporate world – sometime in the August of 2019 – I received a call from an excited Gaurav. He congratulated me on an article I had written about my college life. On BITSians Day (celebrated annually on the first Friday of August), it was shared on BITSians for Each Other – a Facebook group with over 35,000 alumni – and met with an overwhelming response. Alumni across batches, even those who had graduated in the 1960s, reached out to me to share their experiences. So I assumed a similar nostalgia had urged Gaurav to ring me up. I was correct, but not quite.

He went on to tell me that over the last twelve months, he had met some of his idols – twenty-two of them, to be exact. Just three to go and he'd be ready.

'Ready for what, Gaurav?' I asked, a bit puzzled.

'A book that you're now co-authoring with me,' he said, without missing a beat.

Thus began the journey of *The Pilani Pioneers*. A book that would take us to Pune, Delhi, Bangalore, Mumbai, and even San Francisco, to meet twenty-five exemplary individuals as we documented their lives and careers. This book has endowed upon us the gift and the responsibility of spreading the message of these pioneers, and for that, we will forever consider ourselves fortunate.

Writing this book provided us with a constant dose of nostalgia. We remembered our last semester in college, when we visited the same old places we had frequented over the past few years. One last time at the Rotunda, at the NAB slope, at ANC, at C'not and our first-year rooms – any and every spot we walked past, sat on, breathed in or even once glanced at. We wanted to take it all in, one last time, a vain attempt at making those days last forever.

This desperation stemmed from something we wanted, needed and dearly loved. The little hamlet that was Pilani had meant so much to all of us; I doubt any of us, even if we wanted to, would be able to forget it for what it was. Who could forget the hubbub of interactions right from day one, with our dear seniors 'selflessly helping us out'. They graciously let us know that at BITS, ragging was spelled i-n-t-e-r-a-c-t-i-o-n-s. The next year, we would also help our juniors with their spellings in the same way.

BITS offers something unique to everyone who arrives at its gates. Some freshers find their clique. Others are stripped of the image of their original selves, which are then rebuilt by the ones around them – both equally beautiful happenstances.

The streams of our lives are inevitably redirected with every conversation.

Most of us were quick to realize that this haven of ours – completely isolated from the outside world with negligible urban activities to keep us engrossed (read 'distracted') – was a blessing. The isolation forced us to turn to people; we talked to, listened to, learned from and grew with them. I hope we stand as one when I say we couldn't be more grateful, for it taught us that we really don't need much. We lost and found ourselves in clubs and departments. It was this catalytic process of delving deeper into our existing passions and/or finding new ones that lifted the fog of 'we came to college only to study'. I can safely say that we came here to do everything, and the studying just happened. The institution educated us, not just about engineering, but also about ourselves.

And man, *did we talk*. All we did was yap about our lives and exchange words. The campus came to life every night – the nexus of morning lectures, the scorching summer sun and messed-up sleep cycles made sure of that. From the NAB slope to the Rotunda, from ANC to C'not, from the Gandhi statue to Patel's, if there was a place to sit, you would always spot us with our lips moving. I bet myself a good fortune that years after graduating, we would remember our time in college and tell ourselves – 'Simpler times, man, simpler times.' And through these conversations, Pilani's offering of nothing gave us everything. This place was eccentric – on some days, everything around us meant nothing, and on others, absolutely nothing meant everything.

It took us more than three years to write this book, and time and again, we asked ourselves why we chose to write about the twenty-five BITSians featured in it and not any other set of twenty-five successful businesspeople. For starters, there isn't an absolute 'best businessperson' scale, and even if there was one, who'd be the judge? Definitely not two twenty-three-year-olds. The common thread that connects these pearls is what they stand for. Apart from being immensely successful in their respective fields, it's their moral fibre that truly brings them and the thousands of BITSians around the world together. Their fields of work may be diverse, but the sentiment of adding value to their lives by giving back to society is distinctly evident in all of them. Abhishek Humbad has done it via his firm, Goodera, which helps other firms manage their CSR; Pradeep Kashyap through Project Shakti, which has helped empower 60,000 women entrepreneurs, and Sandhya Prakash through Beacon – her energy management and solar solutions firm.

We hope that the stories of the trailblazers who rose from this institution fuel your passion to strive for success. If you are a high-school student, we hope this book excites you about college life and beyond. If you're in college, we hope it helps you realize the gravity of these pivotal years, and if you're a graduate, we hope the tricks of the trade mentioned within these pages enrich your life and career.

The town of Pilani may seem an inhospitable place, but for a moment in its long history – for the four years of our lives we spent there – it wasn't. We hope to learn to love like the place loved us – forgiving the flaws, accepting the rest and when it was time, letting go; in other words, 'agape' – love without attachment. This was more than we could have asked for.

# IT'S LIKE LUDO

## Abhishek Humbad, Founder and CEO, Goodera

Abhishek is the founder and CEO of Goodera – a global leader in volunteering, ESG and CSR Management. Goodera enables forty of the Fortune 500, including Apple, Amazon and Novartis, to channelize more than three million employee volunteers and over $500 million corporate social responsibility (CSR) capital annually to thousands of NGOs in 100 countries across the globe. Abhishek holds a B.E. in Electrical and Electronics Engineering from BITS Pilani and an MBA from IIM Bangalore. Abhishek was part of *Forbes'* 30 under 30 list for both India (2014), Asia (2016) and MIT Innovators under 35 (2016).

## First Pitch

WHEN ABHISHEK REJECTED AN OFFER FROM MCKINSEY & Company as a young graduate, in his heart he knew he was doing the right thing. 'The first time I went to their office, I realized I would start at a junior position, and hence, my ideas would have to go through an array of objections in the hierarchy. It's important for me to see my efforts come together and that's the primary reason I didn't join McKinsey.' Though Abhishek agrees that he would have got a great deal of exposure at McKinsey, he doesn't regret his decision because he feels he has got his fair share of exposure now.

Abhishek recalls how raising the first round of funding for his company Goodera was one of the toughest challenges for him. 'It was initially difficult for us to convince our investors because CSR is not the most conventional space. We weren't emulating a concept which already existed and hence, it wasn't "tried and tested". Our business model to make profits while helping non-profit organizations was baffling in itself.' He observed at the time that convincing clients was easier than convincing investors, because they saw the value and merit in Goodera's vision. 'Clients understood that we were solving a big problem for them, and it was helpful for us in the long run, because we had to have actual revenues, product-market fit and good client feedback to get our first round. That time it sounded like a pain, but it was pretty useful.' While the first round of funding led them on an arduous journey, the second round was much easier and successful.

Abhishek admits it's common for an entrepreneur to doubt himself and question his decisions. 'We consider ourselves one of the best teams working in this space, but I have my days of doubts too. I am sure such thoughts come to every entrepreneur. You might be in the hottest industry, and you can still have such doubts. I think it's important to keep these thoughts and keep reflecting on whether you are doing the right thing and what more you can do. Every couple of years, you should try and change the frame of reference. What happens is that if you try and optimize in a particular box all the time, there is a limit to it. Sometimes you just have to change the box and that will lead you to discovering something new altogether.'

## Goodera: Profit, People and Planning

'CSR in India witnesses a cash flow of about $2 billion per annum. As per government mandate, all companies with a net worth of ₹500 crore or more, a turnover of ₹1,000 crore or more, or a net profit of ₹5 crore or more, are required to spend 2 percent of their average profits of the previous three years on CSR activities, every year. The same number in the US in 2019 was more than $500 billion. 'The primary challenge to enter this space was to help firms understand the impact of CSR. Then, we focused on discovering NGOs, and later, on financing. We formulate separate modules for NGOs and the firms related to volunteering, sustainability and CSR. Goodera's vision is to become an ecosystem where empowering the world with good will be our mission. We want to do this by ensuring that there is a proper flow of capital and information, while also engaging stakeholders effectively. This industry is one of the largest global employers, and needless to mention, it holds immense potential.' In other words, Abhishek aims to use tech to alter the way the '1-trillion-dollar doing-good space' NGOs operate globally.

He believes Goodera's impressive performance is because the concept is fairly innovative. 'We bring transparency and measurement to the CSR space while also creating significant engagement activities for the employees of the company. Our decade-long experience in this space has helped us gain valuable insights that we deliver to our clients. When the profits of a company are meticulously planned to create an impact while ensuring people engagement, we feel we would be able to head towards a sustainable planet.'

## Empowering NGOs

'Bigger NGOs pass on donations to smaller ones, which may change hands three or four times before being put to use. At each stage, there will be approximately a 10 percent cut. We wanted to fix that,' explains Abhishek. Goodera also aims to remove the middlemen who help small NGOs connect with established firms in metropolitan cities by putting them in touch with these firms directly. 'We help the smaller NGOs create a profile on our platform which helps them showcase their work effectively so that companies can search and connect with them effortlessly.'

Abhishek speaks highly of the standardization Goodera has put in place for all the NGOs they have partnered with, along with setting up digital payments so that donations are not restricted by physical distance. In addition to this, Goodera has also set up a volunteer management system for NGOs and volunteers to connect and coordinate with each other. 'In short, this allows them to not only access various grants set up by major companies, but also enables them to tap into the pool of resources that accompany these companies.'

## CSR in India

While explaining CSR in India, Abhishek applauds the government's sizeable monetary contribution. 'The government spends thousands of crores across a multitude of sectors such as healthcare, education, women empowerment and rural development. It spends more than eighty thousand crores on primary education alone, which is substantially more as compared to private firms.' Abhishek asserts that private firms can add more value to their CSR initiatives if they move on from simple cash donations. 'It could be their technology, domain of expertise or anything, wherein they can create more leverage from the cash that they are spending.'

With a lot of millennials wanting to work in companies that are more socially responsible, Abhishek believes that this makes companies involve their employees in more engaging ways. 'The CSR sector has become more data-driven, as opposed to it just being a marketing ploy. People now ask you more questions about what you did with the money that was donated. Firms have come to realize that they can't just donate two percent to CSR and run the rest of their business without being socially and environmentally responsible.'

## Attracting Talent

Contrary to the common misconception that working towards goodness is a trade-off wherein one's career suffers, Abhishek feels that Goodera gives employees the opportunity to grow rapidly and work with the best technology, while enjoying a competitive pay grade. According to him, people inherently want to do good and hence, attracting talent for Goodera hasn't been a hurdle.

Their vision has attracted a young workforce to the company and as a millennial, Abhishek feels quite at ease with them. 'We look for people who want to create an impact. We value transparency and communication and respect the "first principles thinking" because we need to constantly solve problems for multiple stakeholders.'

When asked about the changes he has witnessed since he started up, Abhishek is quick to highlight the positives. He feels that parents today have become more receptive to the idea of their child choosing to create a startup instead of accepting job offers from MNCs. 'Stakeholders, too, have become more receptive; even if you fail, it's great work experience. We would love to hire an entrepreneur who continues to be driven, even after his startup has failed. It just goes to show their tenacity.'

Regardless of the outcome, startups are better equipped today. 'You have more resources now, which enables you to iterate quicker, using the fail-fast philosophy.'

Moreover, a young entrepreneur starting out today has a plethora of existing founders to seek help and advice from. 'Only a founder can potentially relate to the most trivial of your problems, and that's why being a part of such a community is vital. I think BITS has a great community. They are always ready to help and that's a huge support.'

## The 10,000-Hour Rule

Abhishek attempts to solve a problem through a two-step process. First, he ascertains whether the problem is worth solving. If the problem seems too complex to invest his time into it, or the return on investment doesn't seem too lucrative, he decides to work on a different problem. If the problem seems worth solving, he makes deft use of the '10,000-Hour Rule' by spending his time acquiring in-depth domain knowledge of all parameters related to the problem.

'There are several layers to this. You need to feel deeply about a certain problem to solve it and the next thing is that it needs to align with the goal. You will run into various kinds of challenges, a lot of them would be such that have never been encountered before, but if you are passionate about solving the problem, you will solve it. You could try to find a problem that is big enough and depending on the impact, decide which problem you would like to solve. The 10,000-Hour Rule is also about how much value you can actually create, but sometimes I think that people do a lot of analysis and don't start at all. If you feel strongly about something, you would be willing to put those 10,000 hours into it. You just need to feel for it emotionally.'

## Be a Maverick

'Be fearless, be shameless,' says Abhishek reflexively. He advises the young guns to be unabashed and not to stall realizing their ambitions. 'You also have to understand that you'll have to toil if you want to be successful. There is no way around it. You might go on for months without making any headway, but you'll have to keep at it. Persistence does the trick,' says Abhishek and goes on to urge the young blood to not draw comparisons with their peers. 'There will be times when you'd be working diligently while your batchmates would be having a blast. Stop right there – these comparisons will do you no good.'

The Goodera founder believes having a mentor is a game changer. 'It gets very lonely and you can't share things with everybody. That's where a great mentor steps in and helps you find your path.' Abhishek emphasizes the criticality of interacting with other founders. 'You get to learn from their mistakes and achievements. When it comes to co-founders, it is important that you gel with them. Ideally, the founders must have complementary skill sets to function like a well-oiled machine through the innumerable ups and downs.'

According to him, the decision to select a co-founder need not be completely objective. 'As the company scales, you need to change a lot individually. You need to transform yourself from a doer into an enabler. Apart from selecting a competent co-founder, one should focus on finding the right investors. Don't go for the highest valuation, go for the people you really connect with, because it's a long-term journey. You need to select people who are great team players.' Abhishek concludes his advice by encouraging young professionals to be mavericks. 'Think crazy ideas – that's how you will usher in change. One cannot pioneer a revolution without madness and conviction. *Koi toh mujhe bola tha ki startup chess jaisa hai. Maine bola, "Nahi, yaar, ludo jaisa hai."* (Someone told me starting up is like a game of chess and I replied, "No, buddy, it's like ludo.")'

## Back to BITS

Goodera's origin story goes back to Abhishek's days at the BITS Pilani campus. His interactions with several alumni made him realize that a significant number of successful BITS graduates worked at Wall Street. This inspired him to found The Wall Street Club at BITS Pilani. 'We also launched an alumni-backed fund, which we could invest in the market to understand how these things work.' It was around this time that Abhishek became interested in carbon credits – tradable certificates or permits which grant a company the right to emit one tonne of carbon dioxide or the equivalent amount of a different greenhouse gas. 'I wanted to apply carbon credits to remote parts of India like Pilani. One such use case was the biogas project that we undertook at Pilani.'

Under this project, Abhishek came up with a process to convert agro-residue to natural gas. Although he was an electrical engineer, he worked on biogas plants for his research paper under the supervision of a professor of chemical engineering. 'After graduating from IIM Bangalore, I started a renewable energy company to power telecom towers. However, we faced a lot of regulatory challenges, so we sold the Intellectual Property (IP) to a large Indian conglomerate, and they are still using it. Nevertheless, working in this space helped us gain a lot of insights. We realized a great deal of money was flowing into the CSR space, yet no one had any clue as to what happened to the money. That's when we thought we could solve this issue by using technology, and that's how we started Goodera.'

# WRITE YOUR OWN SUCCESS STORY

## Abhishek Nayak, Co-founder and CEO, Appsmith

Abhishek Nayak is a tech entrepreneur who is the co-founder and CEO of Appsmith. Appsmith is an open-source web framework that helps companies build internal business apps. He previously worked at Accel Partners as an entrepreneur-in-residence. In 2011, he co-launched GharPay, a payment service that facilitates cash payment collection for online merchants. He graduated from BITS in 2010 with a bachelor's degree in Biological Sciences.

## Testing the Waters

THOUGH ABHISHEK HAD JOINED BITS TO PURSUE A DUAL DEGREE in Biology and Pharmacy, he gradually realized that his interests lay elsewhere. And BITS gave him the opportunity to explore other avenues. 'I wanted to get work experience and at that stage, internships were the way to go about it. During the summer, post my third year, I interned at a consulting firm in Hyderabad. This particular experience gave me an insight into entrepreneurship. Back at the campus, I was also a member of the Centre for Entrepreneurship and Leadership (CEL) club, through which I was able to meet some entrepreneurs.' His summer internship widened his horizons; he claims that this was the first time he felt intensely intrigued by the concept of startups. 'Coming from a working-class family that had never ventured into the field of business, the idea of starting my own business was an alien one, because I didn't really have any motivation then.' However, smitten by the startup ecosystem, Abhishek worked towards being a part of it.

By the time he was in his fourth year, he had acquired an impressive skill set, including coding, writing and designing, which helped him immensely. 'For instance, I used to write for this climate change blog, through which, I was able to make enough money to pay my semester fees. I was also winning money through quizzing. So generating income was never going to be a problem for me.'

## Course Correction

One of Abhishek's most memorable experiences at BITS was travelling to Denmark in 2009 for a United Nations conference, which was attended by the likes of Barack Obama and Manmohan Singh, among other world leaders. 'I was able to travel to and participate in the event with no monetary support, which taught me how to be resourceful. In the same year, I was able to visit Europe some five times, as the conferences sponsored me. These conferences were on a variety of topics like economics, climate change, social issues, among several others.' It was during his travels as a student that he interacted with MBA students from Stanford, Harvard, and various other institutions, which strengthened his resolve to become an entrepreneur. By the end of 2009, he had made up his mind to venture out and build a startup.

Over the next year, Abhishek invested his time and attention into building something that he truly believed would be a fruitful venture. He even dropped out of one of his dual-degree courses (Pharmacy) to work on his cash-on-delivery service startup idea, which would eventually become GharPay. 'By the turn of the year, I, along with my co-founders Arpit Mohan and Abhiram Kasina, had started our business in Hyderabad. We were able to generate revenue from day one, with several companies like redBus and Inkfruit as our customers. Soon, we expanded to Chennai and were able to raise some capital from Sequoia Capital. This was the beginning of my journey as an entrepreneur.'

## A Frugal Founder

As a founder, Abhishek prefers to adopt a resourceful and conservative approach. 'You have to realize that investment and revenue are totally different – you get an investment once and you need to use the funds cautiously. At the same time, you need to think about the return on investment.' He explains how some founders often err in this respect, 'For instance, some startups spend their investments on renting swanky offices. When they are forced out of these places by the landlords, it becomes a massive loss for the startup. An office is necessary to drive employee morale, but if that is the only source of employee morale, then the office is in deep trouble. An employee needs to get a sense of professional growth for himself and also be able to see whether or not the company is growing.'

Abhishek warns that being too careless with money leaves you vulnerable and makes it easy for other people to take advantage of you. 'Some employees are gold diggers, hopping from one venture to another, looking for a pay hike without necessarily working towards upholding the company standards. I believe when founders attract employees who are as frugal as they are, the company tends to do well. Initially, a lot of successful companies also focus on making their customers happy. This will not just influence the interests of people but also increase the amount of money that you generate.' A good founder, according to Abhishek, is one who knows *when* to invest.

## Experience at Y-Combinator

Y-Combinator is a world-renowned American seed money startup accelerator, and Abhishek was a part of the W17 (Winter of 2017) cohort when he was working on his startup idea – bicycle.ai. 'YC is highly acclaimed because of the way it is run – the way the whole organization operates is a sight to behold. It doesn't depend on anyone to drive their leads or traffic, which is a massive concern for most organizations; instead, YC uses its brand to get traffic *from* entrepreneurs. All its operations are software-enabled and when coupled with the consistency with which YC guides budding entrepreneurs, it becomes a formidable force. They have never changed their core philosophy – a startup will be successful if it provides what the people want. It seems like a simple idea, but unfortunately, the average entrepreneur normally doesn't think about it. If you do not have something that people want, then build it. If you have something that the customers want, YC advises you on how to sell your idea. The participants in the programme that YC conducts are highly competitive. This competition naturally drives you to do better and invariably increases the value of YC as well.'

## Startups in the Valley vs Startups in India

'A major difference between the ventures in the Valley and those in India is the size of the markets. American startups have a significant advantage in that they function in a larger market. When it comes to entrepreneurial skills, you can't really differentiate between the two.' Abhishek feels that Indian startups tend to be influenced by western culture, but such imitation doesn't ensure similar success, as India is a much tougher market to crack for startups. 'It is more demanding than the US markets. On the brighter side, this does uplift the quality of the products. Indian founders excel when it comes to the rate at which they function. They operate more swiftly and decisively. Indian techies are significantly better when it comes to product, application and customer experience.'

Abhishek admits that while Indians think more carefully about products, the American founders have an edge when it comes to communication as well as business experience. 'We tend to figure out our respective career paths considerably later in our lives than the average American does, which reduces the amount of early learning we acquire in a specific field, primarily because we don't have as early a start.'

## Future of Startups

Abhishek feels that 'magic' happens when a disruptive change occurs in an industry that has the right clientele and the right technology to support the change. According to him, fields like blockchain and artificial intelligence are transient in their popularity, and people need to identify the changes that are taking place in their field of choice. 'If you are at that cutting edge, you'll never be short of insights. You will always be a step ahead of the pack.'

It's evident that Abhishek is a proponent of the first mover's advantage when he tells us, 'You might experience a lot of failures, but you will have unique insights that most won't. People also have to be prepared to think of the future while coming up with something worthwhile. It's similar to being a science fiction author, wherein you are dreaming of tons of different worlds. In this way, you'll always be prepared for any change around you because you have already thought about the different worlds. In other words, one must be able to assess the potential of the content that hasn't made its way into mass media yet. So, there are lots of unknown industries that you need to think about or even dream about, and then venture into them. This is the only way you can have originality.'

Cash on delivery is one such example. When Abhishek first stepped into the startup world with GharPay in 2010, nobody had actually given this service much thought, but by 2011–12, the industry boomed. 'Initially, we were able to set the prices on the delivery because there was no competition and the idea was pretty alien to most people. This was the best time for us to grow as a company because people were willing to accept our prices, and they were comfortable with this style of payment. Staying ahead of the curve paid rich dividends.' While he had many other ideas at the time, Abhishek knew that this was something he could pull off as this service was the most viable one. 'You have to learn to differentiate between new industries and mere fads.'

## Scripting Your Success Story

With experience, Abhishek has realized that being a good founder is as important as being a good investor. 'Being a better investor helps you become a better founder and vice versa. For a person starting from scratch, there are several things you can do. Investing in the stock market is a good place for college students to start. All you need is a PAN card and some money to invest. This will create a culture for people, compelling them to study the fluctuations in markets as well as businesses.' Encouraging college students to get a head start, he says, 'You will be able to understand the long-term trends in markets and it doesn't take a whole lot of time out of your busy schedule. I would also suggest that people buy shares and see how it works. Keep evaluating yourself throughout the process.' Abhishek also recommends finding the time to learn about sales and marketing.

For Abhishek, the common denominator of all success stories is clarity. 'Formulate a definite plan and work towards it, and you will surely be able to write your own success story.' He encourages students to go out into the world and try to gain a range of perspectives. 'It is essential that they go for internships and have at least some work experience in the field that they hope to enter in in the future. The internships taught me that ninety-five percent of employed people are actually unhappy. So, despite getting one of the biggest job offers on graduating, I didn't take it because I knew my heart was elsewhere. I think four years is a lot of time to introspect and test whether you are going to be happy with the decisions you might come to make. Discover your own stories and the rest of your world will definitely fall into place.'

## Back to BITS

Abhishek dearly misses the late-night discussions with his college friends. 'It was with a mix of smart people from different clubs and departments, and I enjoyed it to the fullest. I could relate to people on a variety of topics, and it enhanced my ability to talk to anybody about any topic. It becomes really difficult to build a similar close-knit circle post college.' While it was easy for Abhishek to mingle with any social group because of the diversity of the students at BITS, things are different now. 'As I have grown older, it has become difficult for me to find another diverse and intelligent group of people I can be as comfortable with. When I meet my old friends now, we still get along really well and have really deep conversations. This is one of my fondest takeaways from BITS.'

# KEEP LEARNING, KEEP GROWING

## Ajoy Misra, Former MD and CEO, Tata Consumer Products

Ajoy Misra is the former MD and CEO of Tata Consumer Products. He joined the Tata Group through the Tata Administrative Services (TAS) in 1980 and spent thirty years of his thirty-nine-year career working in various departments of the Taj Hotels – from Sales and Marketing to Operations. He progressed to become the general manager of Taj President Hotel in Mumbai and was then posted in Sri Lanka as the area director of Sri Lanka and the Maldives and the general manager of Taj Samudra Hotel in Colombo. His last position there was as the senior vice president of Global Sales and Marketing for Taj Hotels Resorts and Palaces.

Ajoy is a civil engineer from BITS Pilani and has an MBA from the Faculty of Management Studies, Delhi University. He also completed the Advanced Management Programme at Harvard Business School. He was appointed as the executive director and deputy CEO of Tata Global Beverages and subsequently took charge as the managing director and CEO from 1 April 2014. He is also a member of the board of directors of various group companies.

## The Tata Way

'WHAT MAKES THE TATA GROUP UNIQUE IS THE FACT THAT IT HAS been around for a century and a half, compared to most Fortune 500 companies today which have been around for fifty years or so,' says Ajoy when asked about Tata's distinctiveness. Founded by Jamsetji Tata, the company was based on 'progressive ideals', which did not exist in the corporate world. Ajoy speaks of Tata's heritage with pride when he describes a myriad of healthcare schemes that were designed for Tata employees in Jamshedpur (also known as Tatanagar). 'All employees swear by the Tata Code of Conduct – an ethical roadmap which emphasizes caring for the community and one's colleagues,' explains Ajoy, describing Tata's way of business which assures that their ethics remain intact.

'At Tata', avows Ajoy, 'you can sleep at night peacefully, knowing that you have not been asked to do anything wrong.'

## A Tryst with Disaster Management

Taj Mahal hotel and Taj Samudra – two among Tata's famous chain of hotels – have been the centre of two tragic catastrophes. The former during the 26/11 attacks in Mumbai and the latter during the 1997 Colombo World Trade Centre bombing. Ajoy had been at the hotels during both the tragedies and took charge of the situation immediately.

Ajoy was the area director of Sri Lanka and the Maldives and the general manager of Taj Samudra Hotel in Colombo at the time the bomb went off in the hotel's vicinity. He vividly remembers being thrown off his bed due to the bomb's impact and seeing a mushroom cloud rise from his bedroom window. 'The bomb that went off at the World Trade Centre was less than a kilometre from the hotel. Taj was one of the first hotels which opened its doors to the wounded. We set up a makeshift camp with bedsheets, towels and whatever we could find,' says Ajoy, recollecting a challenging time.

Taj actively worked towards rehabilitation until the local state emergency squad came to help out and set up an instant first-aid centre for all the wounded, including residents and staff of the other affected hotels, which had been in the blast's radius.

In 2008, Ajoy once again found himself amidst an unfortunate terrorist attack at the Taj Mumbai. Ajoy, who was

Senior Vice President of Sales and Marketing, Indian Hotels Company at that time, handled communications and press updates during the horrific attacks. 'I spent that entire night at Gateway of India outside the Taj, ducking bullets, watching explosions go off everywhere.' Ajoy's role within the crisis cell was to see Taj through this calamity and to recover from it while upholding the brand image. He helped set up makeshift call centres to cater to the hundreds of residents and staff members stranded inside the Taj and their worried relatives.

'You obviously couldn't call the hotel and speak to anybody there. We had to assess the number of people trapped, figure out how to evacuate them and determine where to shelter them till the whole crisis was over,' shares Ajoy, giving a gist of his work, which went on non-stop for the next eight days, even after the hotel was handed over back to the management on the third day of the attack. He undertook the Herculean but necessary task to contact the residents of all 550 rooms to return their valuables and assets which had been left behind.

Ajoy mentions it was critical to keep calm, to not ponder over what had happened, but to focus solely on what to do next. The media on the scene wanted answers and the hotel management needed to draft a sensitive and comforting statement to avoid panic at any cost. They needed to be in control and that's what they did. A helpline was immediately set up and the number flashed on national news channels. Ajoy tells us that Tata's admirable response to the crisis that ensured 'nobody left the Taj' in the aftermath, widely acclaimed at the time, is now a case study at Harvard!

## Cultural Diversity in the Workplace

Ajoy finds working with a company that has a British, an American and an Indian presence like Tata Global Beverages – now Tata Consumer Products – to be an exciting challenge. 'We acquired the UK-based Tetley in 2000 and the American Eight O'Clock Coffee Company in 2006, among others in Czech Republic, Poland, Russia and a joint venture in South Africa.' As a global venture, Ajoy explains, the firm's focus is to function as a single unit. 'We want uniformity but we also want diversity to coexist, because at the end of the day you don't want to impose your culture on others.' He believes that Tata has mastered this fine art over the years. 'We adjust and we expect our partners to adjust in return. That's how we have made sure most of our processes, systems and habits remain standardized.'

Ajoy elucidates his point with an example. He feels Indians cherish flexibility, whereas most of the western world spends time in meticulous planning. 'We must adapt to find a balance between retaining the flexibility to adjust in the best interest of the company and getting into a habit of planning in advance.'

Similarly, coordinating across different time zones and work cultures is another challenge when operating on a global scale, observes Ajoy. 'In India, several people start talking at the same time; basically, overlapping conversations are rampant, whereas in the West, decorum dictates that the person speaking is allowed to make their point first. So we make sure to coach our representatives and employees to be sensitive towards various work cultures. There's learning on both sides.'

## Keeping up with Changing Times

According to Ajoy, the marketplace has changed quite significantly over the years. 'Take Information Technology (IT) and digitization, for example. They have transformed the way business is carried out. Therefore, companies that want to stay relevant have to adopt the DNA of technology, whether it is Artificial Intelligence, IoT or the trends that follow,' says Ajoy. Change is the only constant, and this axiom holds true even in the world of business.

## Tata Administrative Services

According to Ajoy, TAS is a unique programme. It is the flagship leadership programme of the Tata Group where young talent is provided with cross-functional opportunities through various industries, organizations and geographies of the Group, giving them exposure and prepping them to become the future leaders that steer the organization. 'I am not aware of any other conglomerate having something similar to TAS. There is IAS (Indian Administrative Services), of course, and then there is TAS. TAS encourages you to move around a lot. In fact, when you first join, for the first eighteen months or so, everybody has to move across five companies and pick up assignments. Working on different assignments in several firms early on in your career gives you a good sense of what that business is about,' explains Ajoy.

He mentions that at the beginning of the programme, the whole batch is given the same training at the Tata Management Training Centre (TMTC) in Pune, which includes introductory courses about the Tata Group, essentially the Tata philosophy. Speakers from various eminent organizations are roped in and there's an elaborate orientation and induction programme before you are sent to different Tata companies. It is also compulsory for everyone to work at an NGO which is funded by Tata Trusts.

'In this way, you are exposed to a wide cross-section of opportunities, and the companies get a chance to look at some of the brightest talent. If your profile matches with what they are looking for, you get posted accordingly. Thereafter, you are encouraged in the first ten years to move across at least three companies to diversify your experience. You can choose to settle down in any of those for your long-term career.' Ajoy also tells us about certain annual joint TAS programmes, wherein everybody from different Tata companies comes together, shares their learnings and experiences, and attends the advanced management courses held for them. This programme boosts the chances of a TAS officer getting to leadership positions.

## The Role of a Mentor

During his time as a novice TAS officer, Ajoy found the intra-batch bond to be very strong and when it came to seeking advice and guidance; a senior TAS officer was implicitly viewed as a mentor. 'But suppose you are not a TAS cadre, then more often than not, your boss is the best person to seek mentorship from. There is no secret formula when it comes to choosing your mentor – you just sense it.'

Ajoy explains that one should be able to identify their well-wishers, but more importantly one should become somebody who someone would want to mentor. 'If you are selfish or arrogant, you're unlikely to have well-wishers wanting to mentor you. You have to be sincere, and you have to mean well. You have to first give before you get.' His mantra is very simple: 'You have to do something good for somebody, be helpful to somebody, for that person to help you in turn.'

## Guiding Light

Speaking like a true Tata man, Ajoy asserts the importance of upholding integrity and being honest. 'There will be times in life when you might get tempted, but never budge, never lie, and never ever try to deceive,' insists Ajoy, who is grateful to the Tata Group for never allowing a situation which could corrupt its employees.

Ajoy advises the younger generation to never become arrogant. 'If you're the smartest person in the room, find another room. Always have the desire to keep learning, to keep growing, keep reading and always ask for more opportunities, especially early on in life. Strive to stay ahead of the curve.'

## Back to BITS

Ajoy visited the campus recently and returned with freshly, treasured memories of his alma mater. He confesses his love for the central lawns in front of the clock tower and compares its appeal to that of Bombay's Oval Maidan and New York's Central Park. 'Sometimes, even in the hottest of summers, it used to be cool outside at night, so we used to take our rugs outside and sleep on the lawns,' recollects Ajoy. No wonder he is not a fan of the New Academic Block (NAB) being built in place of the lawns.

'My fondest memories are of the calm and peaceful Birla Mandir. I am not that religious, but I would just love the feeling of going there, taking off my chappals, sitting in one of the corners of the temple on the cool marble floor in the warm summers, reading a book, just spending a few moments by myself.' Ajoy also used to frequent Nutan – a stall near the Pilani bus stand – for his daily chai and to indulge in some chicken curry or *titar* (partridge) curry, when he didn't feel like having the food available at the mess – which he says happened quite often. If not at Nutan, he could be found at the *redis* beside the hostels at BITS. These small makeshift stalls have been serving samosa, Maggi, orange juice and other easy-to-prepare food for the past thirty years. 'We loved snacking at the redis – the food was great, and they served us meals on credit.' Ajoy remembers the library's book collection as 'quite extensive' and being fascinated by the computer centre that had just come up. 'The computer ran on Fortran IV (a programming language). Back then, writing a simple program like one to convert Fahrenheit to Celsius used to be a huge task. So many cards had to be punched and put into this huge mainframe to get an output.'

His keen interest in aviation led him to opt for the gliding courses offered by Birla Gliding Club in Pilani. 'The courses were a bit expensive, but the experience was good fun. There was a mechanical winch that would tow the glider to the jeep along the clayed strip, and you would sit in the glider with the trainer. The glider would be pulled along and once the plane would take off, the tow line was taken off. Your goal was to level the glider using the tail wing, the fins and the wings to manoeuvre it,' describes Ajoy, relishing the memories of his gliding lessons.

A college jock, Ajoy also took part in almost every outdoor sport BITS had to offer. 'My friends and I loved going for hikes in Rajasthan every three months or so. We would cycle down for hours and come across some abandoned fort or havelis, camp there and mingle with the villagers. Pilani had a unique charm of its own as a campus in Rajasthan,' recounts a nostalgic Ajoy describing his adventurous college days.

# NO SHORTCUTS

## Arun Bajoria, President and Director, JK Tyre & Industries Ltd

Arun Kumar Bajoria is an eminent corporate leader with an illustrious career, spanning over five decades. A distinguished alumnus of BITS Pilani, he graduated from the college in 1964. Today, he is Director and President of JK Tyre & Industries Ltd and has led the company by successfully completing key acquisitions, transforming business processes and integrating teams both in India and abroad. He served as a member of the Board of Governors of the Madhav Institute of Technology and Science (MITS), Gwalior, for nearly three decades. The founder president and charter member of the Rotary Club of Birla Nagar in Gwalior, Mr Bajoria has been honoured with the Paul Harris Fellow Recognition for his regular contributions to the Rotary Benevolent Fund. He enjoys travelling and has been to nearly fifty countries. His other interests include swimming, photography and music.

## Early Days of Career

AS A STUDENT, ARUN BAJORIA USED TO RECEIVE ₹250 EVERY month from his father. He used to manage to save enough to write postcards to several educational institutions in the US seeking admission into a postgraduate program with a scholarship. He was all set to move to the US for his postgraduation after securing a scholarship to Stanford University. However, his maternal uncle strongly advised his parents against the move, claiming that if he was allowed to live abroad at the young age of twenty, his parents might never see him again. 'That was the end of my dream of studying at one of the world's best educational institutions. To his credit, my maternal uncle offered to take me along with him to Calcutta, where I was sent for an interview for an entry-level role as Apprentice Officer for the Graduate Training Programme at Texmaco – a hydroelectric power generation company. The interviewer was the legendary industrialist Shri K. K. Birla ji!'

On being asked whether he would like to continue the interview in Marwari, Hindi or English, Mr Bajoria humbly replied that he would prefer English but was fluent in all three. That seemed to seal the deal. While discussing the salary, Mr Birla explained that there were only two grades in his prestigious organization. They offered ₹450 per month to graduates with first division and ₹350 per month to those with second. To Mr Bajoria's delight, his illustrious academic record got him ₹450 and a single-room accommodation in a brand-new building.

## Cimmco in the Seventies

At a chance meeting in Calcutta in 1969, Mr Bajoria met D. P. Mandelia – a close confidant of BITS Pilani founder, Dr G. D. Birla. 'Shri Mandelia offered me an opportunity to further my career at Cimmco – a textile machinery manufacturing company of the Birla Group in Gwalior.' Mr Bajoria decided to take the leap and shifted to Gwalior in October 1969, to become the youngest vice president of Cimmco, Birla Nagar.

The initial years were full of struggle as Cimmco was not doing well and incurring losses. But with hard work, grit and determination, Mr Bajoria was able to turn the company around into a profitable entity within a short span of time. He focused on optimizing resources, reducing non-yielding overheads and hired a competent sales and marketing team. Detailing the concrete steps taken for the company's success, he says, 'I also spearheaded three joint ventures, including Dornier and Karl Mayer in Germany and Toyoda (the famous Toyota car manufacturers) in Japan. This enabled Cimmco to introduce the latest weaving machinery technology. Soon enough, they began manufacturing Dornier's latest shuttle-less weaving machines and Toyoda's air-jet looms, which would become very popular among textile mills in India.

## Life Has Its Own Plans

After a long tenure of nearly thirty-three years with the Birla Group in Calcutta and Gwalior, Mr Bajoria took up a new challenge and relocated to Mysore to step in as President and Director of Vikrant Tyre in 1997. This loss-making venture had recently been acquired by the JK Tyre Group from the Government of Karnataka. 'With guidance and support from Dr Raghupati Singhania ji (Chairman and Managing Director, JK Tyre), I played a key role in grooming the new management team, streamlining operational processes and turning around Vikrant Tyre into a profitable unit within fourteen months.'

In 2003, Mr Bajoria took up the mantle of JK Tyre as the president of the company and was put in charge of pan-India operations. From the company's Delhi office, he oversaw an impressive growth in revenue from about ₹1250 crore to ₹10,000 crore while the market cap skyrocketed from ₹114 crore to nearly ₹2,500 crore.

## Taking JK Tyre International

Under Dr Singhania's visionary leadership, JK Tyre acquired an ailing tyre manufacturing company, Tornel, in Mexico in 2008. Mr Bajoria was entrusted with the responsibility to turn it into a profitable entity and transform JK Tyre into a truly global brand. It was while heading the Mexican firm that Mr Bajoria worked with and ran a foreign enterprise for the first time. 'Tornel gave JK Tyre closer access to the North and Latin American markets. Today, JK Tornel is an original equipment tyre manufacturer and supplier to some of the world's best automotive companies and is also well known for manufacturing passenger car radial tyres in Mexico, Brazil and the USA. It is always a proud moment for any Indian to see JK tyres fitted on Nissan yellow taxis in New York,' shares Mr Bajoria who considers this acquisition to have been a huge stride forward for JK Tyre.

More recently, in 2016, he was given another opportunity by Dr Singhania to acquire Cavendish Industries Ltd (erstwhile Birla Tyre unit at Laksar, near Haridwar, Uttarakhand). With this acquisition, JK Tyre, which was primarily known for its leadership in the truck and bus radial tyres segment, was able to expand its market reach to include the desired two- and three-wheeler tyre range. This, Mr Bajoria attests, has boosted JK Tyre's capacity across twelve plants – India and Mexico included – with thirty-three million tyres being manufactured per annum.

## Lifelong Learner

Mr Bajoria emphasizes the importance of being curious, and suggests that regardless of one's age, one should always be open to new experiences. A lifelong learner, he has never passed on any opportunity to pick up new things. In 2006, he enrolled in the Advanced Management Program in Strategy and Leadership at the London Business School. He has also participated in the JK Strategic Leadership Program conducted by the Harvard Business School. 'I also had the honour of attending the International Advanced Learning Program on Mergers & Acquisitions at Wharton Business School, University of Pennsylvania in 2013,' says a grateful Mr Bajoria.

## I'll Sleep When I'm Dead

Mr Bajoria is famous for his tireless work ethic and is also known for devoting twelve to fourteen hours a day to his job. Once, when he was asked by a reporter about his fifty-year-long career, he pointed out that seventy-five years would be a more accurate figure. To relieve the puzzled reporter, he explained, 'An average professional works about eight hours a day. Since I work for twelve hours, isn't it correct to multiply my career by the same factor? I started my career as an apprentice officer at Texmaco in January 1965. I put in the same hours even today, after fifty-six years, as the director and president of JK Tyre & Industries.'

But Mr Bajoria also realizes the importance of unwinding and relaxing after work. He has an array of hobbies to help him do so. 'I am fond of listening to music, watching movies, going out for drives, photography and travelling. I see great value in undertaking social work. It's a win-win situation for me if I can give back to society and find peace and happiness through it.'

## Gyaanam Param Balam

Mr Bajoria has actively engaged in social work by supporting and serving educational institutions across the country. 'I am a board member of Madhav Institute of Technology and Science – a leading engineering college in Gwalior with over 4,000 students. I am also a member of the managing committee of Lakshmipat Singhania School, Jaykaygram, Rajasthan, and was a member of the executive committee of Technological Institute of Textiles, Bhiwani, Haryana till 2010.' Apart from this, he also has the distinction of being a Fellow of the Institution of Engineers and Guest Faculty at Jiwaji University, Gwalior and Mysore University. He founded the Rotary Club of Birla Nagar in Gwalior, and his immense contributions to the Rotary Benevolent Fund earned him the Paul Harris Fellow recognition by the Rotary Foundation based in the US.

As a member of the Executive Committee and Managing Committee of Pushpawati Singhania Research Institute, one of the leading multispecialty, 200-bed hospitals in New Delhi, Mr Bajoria has also assisted the institute in rendering world-class medical services to its patients.

Mr Bajoria also invests significantly in various philanthropic initiatives, which include scholarships for the underprivileged, establishing and running schools and hospitals, among others. He is proud to share that his granddaughters have taken after him in this respect. 'It is a pleasure to see my granddaughters wholeheartedly participate in meaningful social work initiatives.'

## Being True to One's Path

From the very beginning, Mr Bajoria has been a teetotaller and a strict vegetarian. He also avoids smoking. A man of conviction, Mr Bajoria has never been one to succumb to peer pressure. He recollects how as a first-year BITSian, at a gathering of close friends, he was asked to smoke a cigarette. 'When it came to me, I outrightly refused to smoke. Initially, my friends were offended, but when I offered to leave the group instead, they came around and agreed to make an exception and let me stay on my chosen path. I have stayed in touch with these friends for nearly sixty years, and even though we live in different parts of the world, our bond that developed in Pilani has only become stronger with time.'

Mr Bajoria's belief in his values and himself have helped him navigate through his life and career. He agrees that there is no shortcut to success and no alternative to hard work. 'You have to be goal-oriented in life. This is a sure-shot mantra for success. There will be times when you feel that a certain goal is not within reach. Don't adjust the goal; rather, adjust your actions.' Mr Bajoria encourages young professionals to be ambitious in life. 'You have to believe that there are no problems big enough, or obstacles challenging enough, to stop a strong-willed, diligent person. No one, apart from yourself, has power over you. Believe in yourself with all your heart, and remember that nothing great was achieved without passion.'

## Back to BITS

Mr Bajoria stepped into BITS Pilani at the turn of the sixties after completing his schooling from Scindia School in Gwalior. In 1964, Birla Institute of Technology and Science was incepted as an institute by Founder Chairman Dr G. D. Birla with the aid of the Ford Foundation Grant, in association with the Massachusetts Institute of Technology. Mr Bajoria was thrilled to get admission into BITS. He shares, 'Ours was the first batch after BITS started its collaboration with MIT. I fondly cherish those memorable four and a half years I spent in college. I graduated with a first-class B.E. (Honours) Mechanical Engineering degree.'

A true all-rounder in college, Mr Bajoria not only devoted time to his studies but also participated in extracurricular activities. He was a member of the music club and the captain of the BITS tennis team and the Birla Gliding Club. He proudly shares that he won the spot-landing championship twice as a member of the gliding club. 'I have such pleasant memories of flying gliders and evening visits to the Saraswati Mandir,' shares a nostalgic Mr Bajoria.

# FORGING SUCCESS

## Baba Kalyani, Chairman and MD, Bharat Forge Ltd

Mr Baba Kalyani is the chairman and managing director of Bharat Forge Ltd and a member of the Prime Minister's Science, Technology and Innovation Council. He has served as the co-chairman of the India-Japan Business Leaders' Forum and the India-Sweden Business Roundtable and the chairman of the National Manufacturing Council, Confederation of Indian Industry. He is a member of various forums, including the US-India CEOs' Forum, Indo-French CEOs' Forum, India-UK CEOs' Forum, World Economic Forum and India-Israel CEOs' Forum. He is the founding president of the Society of Indian Defence Manufacturers and the founding chairman of Pratham Pune Education Foundation.

In 2008, he was awarded the third-highest civilian award in India – the coveted Padma Bhushan. He has been bestowed with international awards as well, including the Order of the Rising Sun, Gold and Silver Star (2019) by Japan; Commander First Class of the Royal Order of Polar Star (2010) by Sweden; Cross of the Order of Merit (2012) by Germany; Knight in the Order of the Legion of Honour (2011) by France and Forge Master at the 20th International Forging Convention (2011). He is also the recipient of the Lokmanya Tilak National Award (2019).

Mr Kalyani is the recipient of the Distinguished Alumni Award (2011) from BITS Pilani, where he pursued his undergraduate degree in Mechanical Engineering. He also has a master's degree from Massachusetts Institute of Technology.

## Days in Karad

'GROWING UP IN KARAD (IN MAHARASHTRA) DURING THE 1950S was a unique experience. The town didn't even have electricity when we first shifted there,' says Mr Kalyani, reminiscing about a time that seems alien to him today. He fondly remembers visiting a lantern-manufacturing factory in Karad as a child. 'It carried out two processes – glass blowing and sheet metal fabrication. It was pretty simple, nothing very complicated, but they had a few thousand people working there. It was largely an agricultural town. So, most of the time, the focus of our attention was on the farms. My father used to have small farms.'

But the town lacked a good education system. 'I studied in Marathi-medium till fourth standard, because the town didn't have any English-medium schools at that time. I moved to Belgaum (in Karnataka) to study in St Paul's School, and less than a year later, moved to Pune to study at the National Model School, which was operating from Aga Khan Palace at that time. The horse stables there were converted into hostels. I wasn't too comfortable there because I didn't know anybody in Pune. My mother is from Belgaum, so she decided that I better return to Belgaum to study, and that's when I joined King George's School there. I finished my Senior Cambridge examinations from there in December 1964, before joining BITS Pilani in 1965.'

## Leading Bharat Forge

When Mr Kalyani joined Bharat Forge in 1972, things were not looking good for the company. He recounts, 'At that time, Bharat Forge was running in losses. I could notice the stark difference after having returned from the US, where industries operated more efficiently. So, the first part of my journey was to fix that problem in six months and then almost every year for the next five years, to double the revenue. In five years, our revenue grew from ₹3 crore to ₹30 crore, and it continued to remain on the rise. All it required was a bit of technology, technical discipline and a little planning.'

Mr Kalyani then set up a steel plant in Pune in 1973. 'In those days, no private companies were allowed to manufacture steel. But this changed with a constitutional amendment that came into force in 1975. According to that amendment, if your total investment was less than ₹1 crore, you could set up a steel plant. For reference, it takes ₹50,000 crore to set up a steel plant today and we had set up a steel plant then with just ₹99 lakhs. We were a small establishment with an inexperienced workforce. I had to work double shifts to manage two businesses simultaneously. I feel that's how I transitioned from a manager to an entrepreneur, learning a lot in the process. Setting up two more plants – one manufacturing axles and the other producing brakes – both as joint ventures, was again a huge learning curve.'

Mr Kalyani had anticipated that an independent axle manufacturer would be in demand soon. 'But, that demand really came a decade after the plant was set up. So the first ten years were very difficult. We had made investments but with no business at hand, we were just leaking money.'

In the late 1980s, Mr Kalyani expanded his forging business and started exporting to Japan, Russia and Poland. 'Exporting was a new learning altogether. You need to pack it right, make sure it doesn't rust, and ensure it is shipped on time.'

## Leap of Faith

Mr Kalyani is well known for his business bravado. One such famously bold decision was made by him in 1989, when he planned to completely automate Bharat Forge's manufacturing processes. 'In forging, there are two crucial parameters – time and temperature. A material put in the furnace to be heated needs to be taken out at a precise time. If our staff would go for lunch and come back half an hour late, the material used to get metallurgically burnt, leading to a subpar output. That's when we started these modernizing exercises.' Bharat Forge was valued at ₹100 crore then, but they had to spend around ₹120 crore in capex (capital expenditure) to bring about the change. 'If we had gone wrong, the company would have gone under. There were several articles written about me at that time, in the financial newspapers, saying that I had made decisions that would ruin this company. Fortunately, I was able to prove all of them wrong.'

## Why Diversify?

With the economic downturn of 1995, Mr Kalyani and Bharat Forge were faced with another challenge. Around that time, 80 percent of Bharat Forge's business was from the commercial vehicles manufactured by Tata Motors and Ashok Leyland. 'Simply put, if they sneezed, we used to fall sick. It was a valuable lesson we learnt – to not concentrate our business and clients, and diversify instead.' The economy took seven years to stabilize and it was not until 2002 that the industry came back to the pre-recession level. In the meantime, Bharat Forge geared up for the road ahead. 'In 1998, we had decided that we couldn't simply limit ourselves to the Indian market;

we had to become a global company and aim to be amongst the top three firms in the world within our business sector.'

Bharat Forge witnessed a tenfold revenue growth from 2000 to 2008. The 2008 economic meltdown made it abundantly evident to Mr Kalyani that the world was completely connected and the ripples from what happened in one corner of the world would spread everywhere else. 'We learnt that depending solely on the automotive industry wasn't the best idea and that's when we started focusing on other industries. The target was to earn 40 percent of our revenue from industrial products and our non-auto segments – like oil, gas and power. We achieved that by setting up two plants.'

Mr Kalyani expanded his footprint in Europe around the same time by foraying into the defence sector – which, for him, was a product of his patriotism. 'India got its artillery from Bofors AB in 1984 and some ten truckloads of technical drawings from Bofors, as part of the technology transfer in 1985.' But India's limited technological prowess meant it could not be put into good use then. Later, when Bharat Forge manufactured its first gun in 2012 and demonstrated it to the defence minister, they made it clear that we were capable of producing world-class weapons in-house.

## Innovations at Bharat Forge

When Bharat Forge decided to venture into the defence sector, the firm created a fairly strong research base to build advanced technology. 'This research base now helps create many more technologies and develop several new products. With strong R&D, we also got into oil and gas – an area we hadn't explored before. Because of our commitment, the oil-and-gas business grew close to 90–100 million dollars through export of components to the US.' The innovations pioneered under Mr Kalyani's leadership were well received. One that stands out is the fluid ends for the shale gas fracking industry – a recipient of multiple innovation awards.

'Venturing into electronics and embedded systems has aided Bharat Forge to enter the electrical vehicles segment. We are also working on carbon composites and for that, we have created a division in charge of designing UAVs (unmanned aerial vehicles). Right now, we are specifically focusing on building a UAV for the military to send fifty-kilo loads to a height of up to 15,000 feet. The military needs for medicines and supplies can be easily met through these UAVs, which otherwise take a ridiculous amount of time to be delivered.'

Bharat Forge's innovation portfolio is as diverse as it is impressive. Ranging from a jet engine division to a 3D printing one, the firm has even ventured into nanotechnology, which is being used to develop joint implants in the biomedical and healthcare space.

Mr Kalyani is immensely passionate about technology. 'I like to scour for technology, but something that is adjacent to what we do. First came the venture in the defence industry, because it requires knowledge and expertise similar to our metals business, as manufacturing guns requires forging.' After that, he went about setting up a plant in Hyderabad to make missiles.

'Another area where we used innovation to save costs is in the usage of liquid graphite as a lubricant. Earlier, a lot of it went down our drains as waste, where it solidified and accumulated as a major pollutant. To prevent that, we developed a process to recycle and reuse that waste.' In addition to being environment-friendly, reusing this waste has helped the firm save ₹10 crore annually and, in the process, developed their own catalyst which has multiple other uses. 'India currently imports this catalyst from other countries, but our next business will be around this, and we will provide it to the Indian market at a much lower price, thereby saving on India's import bills.'

'The beauty of our new lines of businesses are that they are built from spillovers from creating our own design in the process. Now if I were to get this product, outsourced I'd probably earn 5 percent, but with my own design, I earn 30 percent from it.'

## Forging Startups

Although Bharat Forge in its entirety may seem like a traditional firm, it has very well managed to keep up with the changing times. 'Presently, we are associated with over a dozen startups. One such startup is Blackstraw.ai which is helping us create and incorporate AI in our systems. We have also supported an electric two-wheeler company – Tork Motors – based out of here, in Pune, which is going to build a full-scale production unit very soon. There are several others whom we support and work closely with, in the carbon composites, inertial navigation systems, IoT, virtual reality and augmented reality spaces,' shares Mr Kalyani with pride. Bharat Forge is a strong proponent of the startup culture in India. Partnering with these startups has given them access to new technologies. 'We are continuously adding knowledge. We are working to put together processes by which these technologies can be converted into products, which can then be sold in the market.'

## Pratham: Education First

A passionate philanthropist, Mr Kalyani founded the Pratham Pune Education Foundation in the year 2000. Pratham provides primary education to underprivileged sections of the local community. 'If you don't care for the disadvantaged, it's going to lead to a society which is full of contempt, not energy.' He explains with an example, 'When I was living in a village, as a kid, we hardly had even 1 percent of the material possessions we have today. But we were a happy society. The ones who were disadvantaged back then were the unfortunate victims of the caste system. But today the political class has created a new divide for their own selfish gains. Today, the slum-dwelling children don't get the same opportunities as urban kids. Although municipal schools provide free schooling in our state, the enrollment rate is still abysmal. One of the things that we have been doing with Pratham for the past two decades is to educate these kids and help them get back to school.' Mr Kalyani notes that most of the underprivileged children who attend school find themselves unable to cope and eventually drop out.

Pratham boasts a brilliant teaching process and syllabus. 'Kids have access to books, libraries and even computers to learn from. We also help young, married women from such communities become teachers here, which helps improve their social standing in their communities.' Mr Kalyani notes that women are the worst affected in such disadvantaged communities. 'Women are regularly abused by their own husbands – who themselves don't work or spend all their money on drinking. Our model solves two problems – puts 20,000 kids into school every year and employs over 800 teachers from the same community that the kids are from.'

Additionally, he has assigned the responsibility of a hundred drought-prone villages in Maharashtra in the past three years to his team, led by Leena Deshpande (Associate Vice President HR and Head CSR at Bharat Forge Ltd) to make them self-sufficient by investing in water-harvesting infrastructure. 'I want these villages to have better connectivity, become cleaner, have better schooling and access to drinking water. We have set specific metrics to help us measure the impact that we are generating in these villages. Because of our efforts, we have managed to double the average income in 60 percent of these villages.'

## Back to BITS

Mr Kalyani remembers being thrilled about joining BITS

Pilani. 'For me, going to BITS was pretty exciting and it wasn't a problem – in the sense that I wasn't leaving home for the first time. I had been away from my house for schooling for almost eight years, and since I already had the experience of living in a hostel, going to Pilani didn't make me anxious. I was excited to go to Pilani, as it was a well-known school. Prithviraj (Chavan) and Pratap Pawar (Sharad Pawar's younger brother) were two years senior to me and were my guardians there. I made many friends in my five years at BITS.'

Not a very 'scholar type of guy', Mr Kalyani was more interested in seeking out adventures at Pilani. 'I learnt from the instructor at the Gliding Club and was able to fly solo after only fourteen flights. I hold this record till date. I was also involved with *Sandy Times*, the newspaper that the English Press Club used to publish.' And in spite of a lack of special inclination towards academics, he was a straight-A student who then courted offers from MIT, Stanford, CalTech and Purdue in his final year at Pilani, finally going on to join MIT.

# KEEP IT SIMPLE

## G. S. K. Velu, Chairman and MD, Trivitron Healthcare Group

Technocrat, serial entrepreneur, healthcare industry expert, Dr G. S. K. Velu is a man with the vision to make healthcare accessible and affordable across the globe by providing cost-effective access to medical technology, diagnostic services, eye care, dental care, super-specialty hospital care and dialysis services. He is currently the chairman and MD of Trivitron Healthcare Group of Companies; chairman of Neuberg Diagnostics, Maxivision Eye Hospitals and director of Apollo White Dental and Apollo Dialysis and Kauvery Group of Hospitals. As an anchor investor at Stakeboat Capital, Private Equity Fund and GSK Ventures, and supports innovations in the healthcare sector.

Dr Velu also holds several key positions in trade associations like CII and AIMED and is Honorary Consul to the Republic of Estonia in India. In February 2021, he was appointed the chairman of the Federation of Indian Chambers of Commerce and Industry (FICCI), Tamil Nadu State Council. He has been dubbed a 'parallel entrepreneur' by *Forbes*, a 'first-generation serial entrepreneur' by many and 'Person of the Year 2018–19' by AsiaOne.

## Humble Beginnings

DR VELU HAILS FROM A HUMBLE BACKGROUND AND GREW UP in Aralvaimozhi, a village in southern Tamil Nadu. In 1984, he made a long journey from the south to study Pharmacy at BITS Pilani.

Explaining how joining the college was a matter of chance, he says, 'I didn't know much about BITS at that time. One of my school seniors had gone to BITS, which is how I came to know about the college. I didn't even know how to fill the BITS form.' There were other troubles too. 'At the time, the college fee was ₹4087. My mother had to give up her *mangalsutra* to put me in college, and we faced a lot of backlash from our relatives, who told us we were wasting our money on private education when government colleges existed,' recollects Dr Velu. In spite of all the misgivings, he has not regretted choosing BITS for his higher education.

## Career Journey

Though Dr Velu aced both the GRE and the TOEFL and managed to secure a seat at IIM Lucknow and Bangalore, his family situation was such that he had to take up a job right after graduation. 'My first job was with IMI, a medical instrument distribution company. My monthly salary was ₹2100. Incidentally, my first salary got pickpocketed, but my boss generously gave me another envelope. In those days, there was no cheque and the salary was given in cash in an envelope. I had dreamt of doing something for my parents with my first salary and I shall remain indebted to my boss forever, because that amount meant more than anything else to me then.'

Dr Velu's thirty-two-year-long career has revolved around medical devices and diagnostics. 'In diagnostics, I became a partner in the same company where I worked, and we floated a company called Allied Healthcare India in 1990 and learnt multiple nuances of the business. However, the most valuable lesson I learnt was never to be business partners with your boss. Although I learnt a lot, I couldn't get any of my shares in the company.' So he decided to return to his corporate career and became a corporate manager of the US-based MNC, Ciba Corning Diagnostics, which later became Chiron. Today, it is a part of the Bayer Group as Siemens Healthineers. 'I actually took up several roles for that company with stints in China that gave me good exposure for setting up a factory and the opportunity to extensively travel to Southeast Asia and Australia, which helped me learn the nuances of the path lab chains.'

Dr Velu started Trivitron Healthcare – a medical technology company providing affordable healthcare solutions – in 1997, and the very next year, he co-founded Metropolis Healthcare, which is now India's leading multinational chain of pathology labs and diagnostics. He went on to spearhead two ventures with Apollo – Apollo Dialysis and Apollo Dental. 'We also operate an eye-care chain called Maxivision. I have tried to replicate my learnings from Metropolis in other verticals. I sold my shares in Metropolis in 2015 and started Neuberg in 2017.' An elated Dr Velu shares that by 2019, Neuberg had already become the fourth-largest diagnostic chain in India. 'We relied very heavily on partnerships because we think you can only grow so much by yourself, but if several like-minded people come together, they can achieve much more.'

## A Simple Man with a Simple Plan

Dr Velu highly values simplicity, honesty and mutual respect. Not one to forget where he came from, he launched 'Pankh' – a programme for underprivileged children – with the motto of giving wings to their careers by educating them at Trivitron. 'I had little money growing up and it was difficult for my family to sponsor my education, but thankfully, my mother could do something about it, and by the skin of her teeth, managed to educate me. There are many families who probably are not able to educate their children, which is why we launched

Pankh – to do our bit for them.' Dr Velu strongly believes that a country's literacy level is the strongest measure of its development and hence wants to work towards strengthening India's education system by expanding its boundaries.

## Scaling Business

The reason Dr Velu has been able to manage multiple partnerships is because he maintains autonomous functioning at all his companies. 'These companies do not have anything in common, not even any financial transactions. They are watertight compartments. I'm the only person in common between Neuberg and Trivitron. While Neuberg doesn't have any external investors, Trivitron has some private equity investors. Apollo is the major shareholder in our dialysis and dental businesses.'

He explains that India imports about 85 percent of medical devices and that is why he spends most of his time at Trivitron. 'I am motivated by the Make In India initiative launched by our honourable Prime Minister and I'm confident that it will yield good results. I am proud to say that Prime Minister Modi inaugurated my Labsystems Diagnostics IVD factory in Chennai, virtually from Mumbai, during the 2016 Make in India Conference and was quite supportive of our work.' Dr Velu has factories in Turkey and Finland, and has received strong support from the respective governments as well. He wishes for India to develop a similar ecosystem for manufacturing as in these countries. 'I could have taken the money I made from my Metropolis business and enjoyed my life but I came back to the pathology business. It's not about the money for me; this is something I'm really passionate about.'

Dr Velu has made significant investments to become one of the largest shareholders in a multispecialty hospital group called Kauvery Hospitals in Tamil Nadu and Karnataka, with over 1,500 beds and 9 hospitals in the network.

## Meeting Dr Kalam

Having interacted a few times with Dr APJ Abdul Kalam, Dr Velu says the late former president always challenged him. 'Dr Kalam was a true polymath. He was thorough with everything and used to quiz me about our new product launches in detail.' Dr Velu claims he has never met anybody as well-read as Dr Kalam. Although he challenged Dr Velu, he also motivated him to do better and to enhance his products. 'He would remember our previous interaction and ask follow-up questions too.'

## Local to Global

When asked about his approach towards taking his ventures global, Dr Velu emphatically asserts that every company should plan to be global. 'You cannot stay local forever, you have to be connected with the world, because it's an information-based economy today. What is happening elsewhere will become a reality here; it is just a matter of time.' He believes that Indians are adept at creating new technology and do so economically, which ensures that every innovation reaches a larger section of the population. He feels making healthcare solutions cost-effective has now enabled Indian firms to become exporters, thereby allowing local firms to become global ventures.

Dr Velu suggests that India needs to design products and services in a globally scalable fashion. 'We might think that 1.3 billion is a good enough population, but that means we are restricting ourselves to an "India only" approach and by the time we launch a product, it might become obsolete for the world,' says Dr Velu, a proponent of 'think global, act local'.

## Investing in Innovation

When asked about what kind of startups he invests in, Dr Velu is quick to share his views, 'I'm excited by ideas that have never been implemented before. I'm not lured by an idea which involves making minor adjustments to something that already exists.' We have two investment wings – GSK Ventures, my family office, and Stakeboat Capital, a private equity firm with a fund size of approximately ₹300 crore. We like to invest in little giants, a term that we use at our office, as the people who we think are little today could become giants in the future.'

Recently, Dr Velu backed a BITSian junior, Harmeet Bindra, who shared his vision for enterprises in the field of pathology. 'Harmeet wants to consolidate dental labs in the US. I funded his idea because I love the concept and see massive potential in it. Since I don't have time to go to the US myself, and one of our fellow BITSians is doing it, supporting him was an easy decision. He has a company called Leixir Resources. It's funded by my family office, as well as by Stakeboat, and it has scaled up very well. Stakeboat is sector-agnostic when it comes to investments; our family office is very healthcare-focused. We also invest through Chennai Angels and Hyderabad Angels – it's good to tag along with experts.' Though he admits to not keeping track of all his investments, he has a dedicated investment team for doing so.

Despite being a pharmacy graduate from BITS Pilani and a PhD in pharmacy, Dr Velu has had no involvement and investments in the pharmacy sector so far. 'Hence, moving forward, the group will look into investments in pharmacy and medical education sectors to become a holistic healthcare conglomerate. With the current group earning annual revenues of over ₹3000 crore, the constituents of the group will grow in parallel to achieve the annual revenues target of $1 billion in the next three to four years.

## Leading by Example

Dr Velu's leadership philosophy, quite like his personality, is based on keeping things simple. 'You can't be the captain and not play the match. You have to lead from the front. Many professionals today, when promoted to the designation of a CEO or CXO, think that they have to stop working and start commanding. The day you stop working, you should retire,' says Dr Velu, with candour. Working with startups excites him because the team members across the hierarchy are equally energetic and diligent. He also follows the triad of belief, positivity and control across all his organizations. 'Believe in what you do, have a positive outlook and commit yourself fully to the task. If you have just these ingredients, you can become a great leader. If you want people to follow you, you should be setting an example and leading from the front.'

## Back to BITS

'The students who join BITS often have a stellar academic record in school, but BITS gives you a reality check when you get your first zero on a test,' says Dr Velu jestfully. He fondly remembers BITS as a peaceful motor-vehicle-free campus and hopes it is still the same. To his mind, BITS was a great equalizer – it did not matter whether one was from Doon School or a village school. He believes BITS helps its students become 'generalists'. He explains, 'Even though you study pharmacy, for example, you also do a bit of instrumentation engineering, a bit of civil engineering, and similarly, gain from a smattering of all other courses.' According to him, the self-confidence and hands-on experience BITS provides its students lays down a strong foundation for the young undergraduates' successful futures.

Dr Velu explains with an example how being a 'generalist' kick-started his career. He went to Adyar Cancer Institute in Chennai for his Practice School-2 (PS-2) to work under Professor Shanta, who was the director of the institute at the time. PS-2 is a mandatory six-month-long internship for all undergraduates at BITS Pilani. During the internship, Professor Shanta challenged the interns to fix a faulty machine in the biochemical department. 'All of my batchmates there had studied different disciplines but had a hint of all branches. We combined our interdisciplinary knowledge and managed to fix that machine,' says Dr Velu, who credits this project for having kindled his passion for biomedical engineering.

'BITS gave you all the freedom and allowed you to take risks. If you don't want to attend classes, it's up to you, but it's your responsibility to pass and use your time constructively. You see more entrepreneurs from BITS than the IITs, and I think it has a lot to do with the freedom and trust BITS offers its students,' affirms Dr Velu.

# PASSION AND RESILIENCE

## Gulu Mirchandani, Chairman and MD, Onida Group

Gulu Mirchandani is the co-founder, chairman and managing director of the Onida Group. He started the flagship company of the Onida Group – MIRC Electronics – Ltd in 1981. In today's highly competitive consumer durables industry, MIRC Electronics has stood its ground by constantly innovating and making products that are sharply differentiated from the competition.

He serves on the board of directors of KEC International Ltd, one of the largest power transmission, engineering, procurement and construction companies in the world. His professional interests also lie in the field of artificial intelligence, big data and analytics. Fractal Analytics, one of his portfolio companies, is a multinational AI and data analytics company. He is also the chairman of IWAI Electronics, a premium audio solutions company and the director of Algorhythm Tech Pvt Ltd, a specialized supply chain solutions company focused on network optimization. In 2019, Mr Mirchandani was honoured with a Lifetime Achievement Award by CEAMA (Consumer Electronics and Appliances Manufacturers Association) for his exceptional contribution to the Indian appliances and consumer electronics industry.

## Sindhis in Business

PROUD OF HIS SINDHI HERITAGE, MR MIRCHANDANI VOUCHES for the Sindhi approach to business. He attests that Sindhis do not shy away from taking risks – a habit that has worked well for them in the field of business. 'I feel Sindhis go to places that others aren't completely comfortable with, or rather, are afraid of going to. Places such as Nigeria, where people won't find the food they enjoy or places with an environment they consider too rough for themselves.' He mentions that there are several markets with a lot of potential and an equally high risk associated with them. 'These markets often don't have any proper laws in place to protect them and big corporate conglomerates might not want to risk entering them, because of this uncertainty.'

Mr Mirchandani also remarks how Sindhis generally adjust well with the local population. 'You need to understand their language to adjust and work with the local population. The 30,000-strong Sindhi community in Hong Kong speaks Cantonese. They're doing very well there, especially in trading. I feel that makes them more adept at managing their business. They make resources available and take tremendous risks.' The Onida chairman's business approach is similar to that of his Sindhi ancestors, as he prefers to venture into unexplored avenues. He is convinced that a market that is dominated by giants cannot be disrupted by a small player. 'You should instead focus on things which no one is working on. For example, I funded a company called Fractal Analytics. Analytics was something none of the giants (Infosys, Wipro, TCS) were working on in the early 2010s, and today, it is a prominent company with offices all over the world. It started from the idea of doing something unique, which the world *needs* in the future.'

## The Onida Odyssey

Mr Mirchandani started his journey with a packaging business – an almost non-existent industry in India in the seventies. 'I wanted to start my entrepreneurial journey with a basic industry to minimize the risk attached to starting with something complicated, such as telecom. I manufactured a cardboard tray for packaging apples.' Since Rondo, a Swiss company, led the world in packaging, he reached out to them for a collaborative manufacturing venture in India. 'In India, Rondo was manufacturing the trays needed for packaging ampoules which were being widely used by several pharmaceutical companies in India. It looked like a basic item but one needed good precision machinery at high speed and consistency to make them and ensure there was no breakage. So I got customers at Glaxo after visiting them nearly thirty to forty times and others, such as Pfizer and Smith, Kline & French. I had about 92 percent market share and nearly 100 percent margins in that business.

Although the packaging business was a profitable one, Mr Mirchandani's father encouraged him to scale up his business. 'With the Asian Games set to be hosted in Delhi in 1982, the Indian government was generously handing out licences for manufacturing indigenous products. I wanted to make a unique product in order to have better margins, avoid competition and ideally, own a monopoly.' And thus he founded Onida – one of the most iconic brands of India – in 1981, along with his partner, Vijay Mansukhani. At Onida, he developed a core competence in sound, which had been a major pain point for Indian customers. Even today, Onida TVs are known for their impressive audio quality in the audio-visual electronics market.

## The Biggest Milestone

Onida began its journey forty years ago with the mission to make Indians proud of the 'Made in India' label. It has been an immensely satisfying journey for Mr Mirchandani. 'The biggest milestone was setting up the Onida factory at Wada in Maharashtra in 1994. It is spread across 57 acres and has the capacity to manufacture 3.4 million colour TVs every year. The three largest companies at that time were LG, Videocon and Onida. BPL was around too, but it shut down and after a while, as did Videocon. Setting up the plant was a Herculean task. It was quite an achievement for us.'

Onida has fared well in the previous millennium, though one particular challenge specific to the electronic industry has always been around. 'Back then, the obsolescence rate in this industry was very high. Today, this problem is not restricted to any particular industry and plagues all of them alike. You have to keep innovating all the time. Technology is changing and you have to keep up.' Mr Mirchandani quotes China as an example of a country once considered backward, which, owing to its significant technological and infrastructural advancements, is now a force to reckon with. 'China kept up with the changing times, and is now leading the world by example.'

When asked about building a sustainable business, Mr Mirchandani's reply was crystal clear. 'A business will surely die if it doesn't have anything new to offer. If the business is unwilling to adapt, it's just a matter of time before it becomes obsolete.' He predicts that brick-and-mortar and e-commerce businesses will probably co-exist in equal partnership because both will remain mutually dependent.

## The *Immovation* Approach

There are multiple factors that have contributed to Mr Mirchandani's success. A beneficiary of the first-mover advantage, he speaks emphatically about the need to consistently innovate. He also believes that the growth of any firm depends on how well it gauges customer pain points. 'If you address the pain point of the customer, you beat the competition. The most important thing is customer satisfaction. You cannot satisfy a customer? You shut down your business,' he says, frankly. 'You should be ready to take calculated risks. A successful venture is built when customer pain points are identified.'

Though a strong proponent of building radically unique products, Mr Mirchandani is also cognizant of the fact that market disruption doesn't happen overnight. In order to attract business, he advises, the service offered should boast a unique selling proposition (USP). 'It's the only way you can differentiate yourself from other products in the same domain.' He proposes the *immovation* approach, which he describes as an amalgamation of imitation and innovation. Much like the nomenclature, this business approach works on identifying a solid product that already exists and then enhancing it with a personal touch. 'Take the iPhone, for example. Apple took the touch feature – already thriving in the smartphone market – and made it much better. They created a state-of-the-art device, superior to the rest, simply by using their remarkable technological expertise. It was only natural that the product would stand out.'

## The Intelligent Investor

Mr Mirchandani prefers to invest in businesses that use minimal physical assets. 'I prefer to invest in a software venture where a laptop is all the infrastructure you need. I like to keep it asset-light, and focus on brainpower.' This means less risk for the business, too. Citing an example, he explains, 'If you think about hotels, say the big American chains, they don't necessarily own the hotels but run hotels owned by some local politicians or rich people. They make a 10 percent margin on it, which is a good business model because the risk is zero. In case the hotel is shut down, then it's the owner's problem, not the chain's. So all these big chains, like Hyatt Regency, Holiday Inn or Sheraton, are fairly asset-light. They own some key hotels here and there in the world, but that's about it.'

Mr Mirchandani also takes great interest in partnering with graduates from top-tier institutions. When it comes to such people, he often takes a back seat and allows them to run the business without interfering and extending his role beyond that of an investor.

## Unwinding

'Everyone needs a stress buster. If you work five days a week, then you *need* some relaxation. Most people just drink, ruin their bodies and go to sleep. I am not a big drinker. I developed this habit of gardening which I find extremely refreshing,' shares Mr Mirchandani who also studies plants and rocks in his free time. He makes it a point to spend time in his garden from six to nine in the morning. 'I have my morning tea in the garden and walk around there. It's not even a hobby anymore, it's truly a part of my daily routine which I look forward to.' Mr Mirchandani visits his property in Khandala every weekend – a greenhouse where he grows orchids. Apart from gardening, he takes an interest in architecture and furniture, and feels that learning about these subjects is 'meditative'.

## The Influential CEO

When asked about what makes a successful leader, Mr Mirchandani replies with unflinching conviction, 'Passion, determination and resilience – the CEO should never give up. In a successful firm, the CEO *must* be an influencer. He should be able to convince people in the direction he wants. Influencing is a rudimentary leadership quality.'

He takes great pride in being able to make people happy by providing high-quality TVs. 'I feel immense satisfaction when customers tell me they have been using Onida products for fifteen years and they're still in top condition,' he says as he explains that a founder's success lies in his content customers. 'I have been associated with consumer electronics for over three decades now. I have enjoyed every bit of building Onida.

If you are truly passionate about something, you, too, can build an iconic brand,' concludes Mr Mirchandani.

## Back to BITS

Mr Mirchandani graduated from BITS in 1965 – a year after the erstwhile Birla Engineering College was rechristened as Birla Institute of Technology and Science – and remembers his stay in Pilani as a 'simple time'.

Recollecting his college days, he remarks about the absence of non-vegetarian food during his time. 'I hear the messes now serve non-vegetarian food? Back in the sixties, the messes didn't even serve eggs,' he chuckles and quickly debunks the urban legend of the rule being imposed by 'Birla ji himself', who apparently spent a sizeable amount of time in Pilani in the sixties. 'That's a mere rumor – Birla ji was rarely around. The rule was actually enforced by the professors. I remember we used to go to the bus stand outside the campus and ask Gupta ji – who used to sell omelettes – to arrange meat for us,' confides a nostalgic Mr Mirchandani. When he joined college, the ID was just a three-digit number, as opposed to the thirteen-digit alphanumeric combination students are assigned today. 'I still remember mine, it was 871!' exclaims Mr Mirchandani, who graduated from Pilani nearly sixty years ago, but whose memory needs no jogging.

# WIN-WIN SOLUTIONS

## Gunender Kapur, Investor-CEO, Vishal Mega Mart

Gunender Kapur started his career as a management trainee with Hindustan Unilever Ltd, where he worked in various roles in sales and marketing – including Marketing Manager, Oral Care India & Dental Innovation Centre (for D&E markets); General Manager, Foods; Foods Director, India; and Senior Vice President Foods, South Asia. Gunender was the youngest manager to be appointed to the Hindustan Unilever board. In 2004, he was appointed as the executive chairman and CEO of Unilever Nigeria. Two years later, he joined Reliance Retail as the president and CEO. He was a part of the startup team at Reliance Retail. In 2010,

Gunender joined TPG Capital as a senior advisor, and TPG Capital acquired Vishal Retail as a part of the Corporate Debt Restructuring programme.

As an investor-CEO of Vishal, he has overseen the company's twelve-fold growth, generating close to $1 billion in revenue. Vishal is a fast-growing, profitable retail business employing more than 13,000 people. In 2019–20, it was awarded the 'NCPEDP–Mindtree Hellen Keller' award for creating employment opportunities for people with disabilities.

## Heading a Firm in a Foreign Country

BEFORE EMBARKING ON HIS JOURNEY AS THE CEO OF UNILEVER in Nigeria in 2004, Gunender had served as the director of the Foods Division of Unilever in Southeast Asia, which made handling affairs outside India relatively more comfortable for him. Working in India, too, substantially benefited him. 'Since it is a diverse country, one gets acclimatized to working in different settings, and thus diversity on a global scale doesn't seem too intimidating.' On the other hand, he found working in a foreign country advantageous in the sense that one notices things that the local communities often fail to. But diversity was nothing new for Gunender, as he mentions getting used to working with a diverse crowd right from his college days.

Over the years, he has realized that despite diversity, people are more similar than dissimilar. 'There are obvious differences in physical appearance, infrastructure and development, yes, but when you look at the people, whether you're from Asia, Latin America or Africa, we are more connected than what meets the eye. We have a similar line of thought when it comes to how people gauge the future, the basic issues that stress people across the globe, and how people prioritize their concerns regarding their safety, health, education.' As for the differences, Gunender shares, 'Personally, I think we are slightly oversensitive when it comes to minute physical differences, which, whether it's a professional or a personal setting, should be ignored.'

At the same time, Gunender acknowledges that one needs to be mindful while expressing oneself in a foreign country to avoid inadvertently hurting someone's sentiments. He emphasizes on the importance of critique in a professional setting for a healthy discussion but advises caution to avoid unnecessary friction.

## Tackling the Unknown

In the face of any unprecedented challenge, Gunender counsels, if one is prepared to embrace different ideas after grasping the basic principles, then trying new ideas and techniques in one's day-to-day life would be a cakewalk. 'Some new ideas might not work out, but it is worth exploring new horizons,' says Gunender, who is reluctant to jump on a different bandwagon. 'I have never been convinced by the idea of taking something up because everybody else is also working in the same avenue, because it defeats the whole purpose of innovation.'

## Supply Chain 101

'Supply chain is vital for every business but its importance grows multifold in the retail side of business as compared to the consumer business. In traditional consumer businesses, the supply chain has become commoditized. Most companies source their products from contract manufacturers. These products are then shipped to the distributors, who sell them to consumers. In most cases, the distributors, transporters and even the contract manufacturers are common.' Having said that, Gunender also sheds some light on the new-age consumer businesses that are trying to step out of this cycle of events and demarcate themselves at the front end at least, if not the back end. The new-age Direct 2 Consumer (D2C) companies, he says, directly ship the goods to the consumers' doorstep to eliminate most steps in the traditional supply chain line, which has become possible due to the recent developments in e-commerce.

'In retail, the supply chain is the heart of the business. In traditional businesses, you buy, move and sell in an integrated way. So, managing these steps is the crux of the supply chain, and hence, people focus immensely on increasing the efficiency of the supply chain, which significantly impacts the business's working capital, the freshness of the inventory, and hence, its financial performance. Incorrect supply chain decisions can obliterate a retail business, whereas a consumer business's success is determined by the product's success.'

## Transformation of Retail Business

A veteran businessman in the retail industry, Gunender observes that organized retail and e-commerce retail businesses are developing parallelly in India, unlike in other developed countries, where organized retail had been established a long time before e-commerce took centre stage. 'All these developments are very positive for one simple reason – if we can make our supply chain more efficient, we can make our products more affordable. Where else would you need this more than India, a country that boasts one of the largest consumer markets in the world? Bringing down the prices for the customer at the front end will trigger consumption and growth of a business, in particular, and the country, in general.'

Gunender describes the paucity of appropriate real estate in India as a huge challenge for retail business. In such a scenario, the use of e-commerce channels to deliver goods and services to the consumer's doorstep is an effective solution. It also provides a means to reach out to the people in areas where a brick-and-mortar model of business is not viable. 'They can now avail e-commerce facilities for both their luxuries and livelihoods. I am extremely excited by the current developments and also by what the future has in store in the retail business.' His enthusiasm eventually led to a partnership between Vishal Mega Mart and Flipkart for home delivery of essentials.

He feels both brick-and-mortar as well as e-commerce are equally important and will continue to coexist in the future. 'If you want to buy clothes, despite the e-commerce facilities available, you sometimes need to try them on. So brick-and-mortar business will stay not just now, but in the future as well. In the fullness of time, I believe they will supplement each other rather than compete with each other,' reasons Gunender, offering an insightful perspective.

## Towards a Pan-Indian Presence

With affordable data services, products and services have become accessible to consumers from both urban and rural regions, in terms of visibility. This had not been true a couple of years ago. So, in addition to reaching out to 70 percent of the subcontinent, under Gunender's leadership, Vishal Mega Mart is now also on the mission to cover the more remote parts of India. 'The challenge for our country now is that while aspirations are becoming the same, affordability is very different. Our mission, thus, is to make the aspirations of these people affordable. It is a very exciting business venture for all employees and customers, which is one of the major reasons why the company has been successful,' explains an elated Gunender.

When asked about the behavioural difference between the average urban and rural Indian consumer, Gunender notes that despite best efforts made by the people and the government, a significant divide still exists in the availability of goods and services, along with employment opportunities, in the two regions. 'The agriculture sector is more prominent in rural India, whereas in the urban areas, tertiary sector services are predominant. Despite these visible contrasting features, urbanization has conveniently assimilated the people from both these regions because of which the differences between them shouldn't be overstated. The rural people aren't marginalized; a few of them just lack social confidence in the urban markets since they haven't been exposed to that environment.'

Gunender believes that with enough time and exposure to brands, every consumer will essentially be the same. People from rural India will develop the same consumer aspirations as those in urban India. Additionally, he feels that despite the literacy rates in rural regions, the customers are in no way subordinate to the urban consumers and the ideas of India and Bharat being different are slightly hyped and overstated.

## Unwinding

When it comes to unwinding from travel and work, Gunender resorts to yoga, meditation and reading. 'My schedule and travels around the world have not been a problem for me. If you are fit, healthy and happy, there isn't really anything to complain about.' An avid reader, he enjoys travelling because it allows him time to read. Another reason he loves travelling within the country is because he feels compelled by the mission at Vishal. 'Every business trip gives us a reason to cheer about possible new opportunities. The fact that so many people within the organization work diligently to make a difference is an energizing feeling and drives you to work towards something special.'

He also finds solace in his spiritual beliefs which he feels are strictly personal but open to be contested by anybody in the world. 'I am not religious, but I am deeply spiritual. I wish I was like that when I graduated from BITS,' he adds with a chuckle. As a twentysomething, he admits, he was driven by the physical world and reacted strongly to external stimuli. 'I am grateful to have discovered spirituality. It has benefited me massively and I recommend everyone to discover their own sense of self. If I had similar guidance when I was young, life would have been so much easier and better.' To Gunender, spirituality doesn't mean that he has achieved mastery over his mind, rather it is about simply being more at peace. 'I try to meditate every day but not for as long as I should. I want to invest more time in it, which is challenging because I travel a lot and I'm at home only on the weekends. Irrespective of that, I still try to take time out of my schedule to invest a few minutes in it.'

## The Indian Startup Ecosystem

Gunender is excited by the developments on the startup front, though he understands that the journey of a startup can be difficult and frustrating. 'It is important to realize that even if one is fundamentally entrepreneurial, it doesn't mean that they will succeed in the startup ecosystem.'

He classifies startups into two categories. 'The first kind is carried forward by enterprising people who are determined, but lack the mental clarity and innovation required to make it big. Startups are meant to solve issues and if they are unable to do so, then the idea behind it becomes futile. The second kind of startup is one that has people who aim to solve an issue, whether it be supply chain for consumer businesses, retail business, or something else. These startups make a deeper impact and live up to the definition of what a startup actually is.' Gunender admits to being biased towards the second type of startups – the ones that focus more on issues than on creating a brand.

Appreciative of the startup culture, he feels they provide a brilliant opportunity for intelligent minds to come together and make a difference. 'In the past, you could only become a successful businessman if you were born into a business family. Now, times have definitely changed as financial resources have become available to everybody. So, it is a really exciting time to be an entrepreneur.'

## Word to the Youth

A proponent of building constructive habits, Gunender feels being consistent has paid him dividends in his professional career. 'If you want to create something concrete and sustainable, you have to be at it from day one.' Being relentlessly at the grind with a fair degree of clarity has helped Gunender achieve his personal and business goals. He makes it abundantly clear that he is not convinced that overnight success stories lead to a win-win scenario for the business and its stakeholders. Gunender has witnessed a lot of people getting stressed out by the fact that they are unable to meet their goals and for that reason alone, have diverged from the path that they initially set out on. 'This scenario, more often than not, will not satisfy these people and leave them wondering about the what-ifs. I used to set deadlines to achieve my personal goals by a specified time, but then I realized that until I'm clear in my mind and determined, it doesn't matter. I'm able to enjoy the process and also ensure that I'm not constantly under unwanted and undue pressure.'

Gunender advises the young guns to sift through their priorities and focus on a select few. 'Honesty is the best policy in creating sustainable businesses and being a good human is critical to being a good leader. *Not one of us can be as good as all of us* – I believe that's the law of the universe. Co-creation is the best way to create,' he generously shares some of the essential principles he has lived by all his life. While Gunender agrees that it is easy to get swayed by competition to create a win-lose situation in one's favour, he is quick to suggest a better alternative: 'Win-win solutions are the only sustainable solutions.'

## Back to BITS

'I appreciated it more when I couldn't experience it anymore,' says Gunender as he dons his nostalgia-tinted glasses. For Gunender, life on campus had been a carefree time as he preferred to live in the moment. 'In hindsight, I believe that the entire experience was amazing. Had I reflected upon my college life at the end of first year, I believe I would have valued the rest of it even more.'

Gunender fondly remembers movie screenings in the auditorium on Saturday nights – one of the few modes of entertainment during that time. With a wistful smile, he talks about spending time with his friends at Connaught Place (or C'not, as referred to by BITSians) – one of the most vibrant spots on campus. 'Irrespective of the kind of day you'd had, you somehow always ended up at C'not.' Another constant in Gurender's life at BITS was his weekly visit to the on-campus Saraswati temple. I used to go to the temple once a week – it was a serene environment. 'In the midst of everything, the Saraswati temple was my go-to place to get a moment of silence.'

'Leaving the comfort of my home was difficult, but all in all, I had a wonderful time at BITS,' concludes Gunender.

# BELIEVE IN YOURSELF

## Hari Menon, Co-founder and CEO, BigBasket

Hari Menon graduated from BITS Pilani in 1983. He started his career with ORG Systems, subsequently moving on to work with many of the best and most-respected organizations in the country, including TVS Electronics, Wipro Infotech, Planetasia.com and Integrated Data Systems. He was also the CEO of IndiaSkills – a vocational education joint venture by the Manipal Education Group and the UK-based City & Guilds.

Hari's entrepreneurial journey began in 1999 when he co-founded Fabmart, one of the pioneers of e-commerce in India and its physical extension, Fabmall, a chain of grocery stores in south India, which was acquired by Aditya Birla Group in 2006 and renamed More.

He is currently the CEO of BigBasket, a company he co-founded in December 2011 with a vision of setting up India's finest online food-and-grocery delivery company. BigBasket has received widespread recognition, including awards at the prestigious Coca Cola Golden Spoon Awards 2016, Global eCommerce Summit Awards Barcelona in 2017, AWS Mobility Awards 2017 and Business Standard Annual Awards 2019.

Hari was also awarded the Distinguished Alumnus Award in 2017 by BITS Pilani for his extraordinary contributions as an entrepreneur. He serves as a Governing Council member of BITS School of Management (BITSoM). A fond lover of music and cricket, he plays the guitar and used to perform with his rock band, The Thunk, at BITS.

## A Breezy Childhood

HARI SPENT HIS CHILDHOOD IN KALANAGAR, BANDRA EAST, AND appreciates being a part of an inclusive society during his formative years. 'I spent most of my time outdoors, engaging in physical games and activities. I don't see this happening as much today, thanks to all the gadgets. We were lucky – we would just go out, play games, be with friends or watch movies at the theatre. Thankfully, I did not grow up in an overly protective environment,' shares Hari. He credits the independence he enjoyed as a child for having made him a better 'decision-maker and risk-taker'.

## Internet Companies in the Nineties

After graduating from BITS, Hari worked at ORG Systems, a computer hardware firm. The way IT companies functioned in the 1990s was not the same as they do in the contemporary scenario. He started his career in 1983, but it wasn't until 1997 that he had an email account. Hari explains, 'When we joined IT, it meant hardware.'

In the absence of immediate connectivity offered by personal mobile phones and the internet available today, Hari says that the work environment used to be quite different. The stress was considerably less, too, which enabled a healthy work culture and lifestyle. 'We had deadlines but not as strict as they are nowadays, like when you receive an email, you are expected to respond immediately. Email IDs were anyway reserved for the privileged few. Wipro had a joint venture with BT (British Telecom) and BT created email IDs only for some top-notch management people. It was a long email ID which no one used.'

When he joined Planetasia.com – one of the earliest internet service companies in India – they were attempting to shift the marketing model from TV and radio to the internet. 'We had to learn everything about a website – what it is and how it's built. Within a year, the cost of building a website from scratch was reduced from several lakhs to just ₹5,000.'

While it may not seem so today, Hari admits, consumer education was tough back then. 'We were selling websites and intranet solutions, but everything was new, so our customers had a difficult time understanding the products we offered and how they benefited them. For instance, we were helping HRs build a workflow for leave management, which meant that employees would just have to fill a form, send it to HR and the database would be automatically updated once their boss approved the leave. It might seem very straightforward today, but those were the nineties when the majority of the operations were done manually and convincing customers about new technology was an uphill task.'

## Eureka Moment

In 1999, a meeting with a leading bank sent Hari and his Planetasia colleague, V. S. Sudhakar, on an entrepreneurial journey to build Fabmart, their first e-commerce website. 'At that time, the bank had floated a tender to all the IT companies to build India's first payment gateway. However, we pointed out that it was pointless to build a payment gateway when there was no transaction website to use it. The bank's plan was to build a shopping website, onboard a few merchants and evangelize the concept. However, after a month, they received instructions from their head office in the US that as a bank, they couldn't involve themselves in this business.'

That's when Hari and Sudhakar decided to build it themselves and the result was Fabmart. 'It was difficult for us to convince our families that we wanted to leave our well-paying jobs to create a shopping site – a risky venture because something like it hadn't been done before. There was considerable resistance, but my wife stood by my decision. I have always considered her to be my mentor and her confidence in me was the tipping point.'

## Development of E-commerce in India

When an entrepreneur in India sold his company IndiaWorld Communications to Satyam Infoway in 1999, the promoters made a few hundred million dollars. This was unprecedented in India as it was the first time promoters had made significant returns in the internet space. 'It created an absolute frenzy and within no time, hundreds of companies founded by young college grads started springing up. As long as you had a ".com" in your company name, you got funded,' Hari jokes. Around this time, when the internet craze was alive and kicking, Hari had counted eighty-three '.com' hoardings while travelling from Bangalore to Mumbai and from the Mumbai airport to Nariman Point in a cab.

But the trend was not conducive to the survival of online enterprises. 'The trouble started later that year, when the country had hundreds of companies, but no ecosystem for internet businesses. We were on dial-up lines, so by the time a webpage loaded, you could actually go, have a cup of tea and come back. It was that slow. Since there was no payment gateway in place, customers had to disclose all their card details to the back-end team, which would authorize the transaction,' says Hari, explaining how unsafe online transactions were at the time.

As a result, companies started collapsing and the entire venture capitalist community gradually realized that this ecosystem was not ready yet. They didn't have a sustainable business model because they were built on an advertising income model rather than a transaction business model. For an advertisement income model to work, one needs scale and customers and given the low internet penetration at that point, the failure of these businesses was inevitable. Fabmart managed to pull through the crisis because they were selling tangible goods, but even then, they barely made any profits.

In a pivotal move to ensure Fabmart's survival, the online company metamorphosed into Fabmall – a physical grocery store – in 2000. Hari considers himself fortunate to have had the right co-founders who suggested switching to a brick-and-mortar business and convinced him that it was the right decision. By 2006, Fabmall had inaugurated 210 stores and thereafter, was acquired by the Aditya Birla group. With Flipkart's debut in 2007 and the popularization of smartphones, broadbands, payment gateways and the internet, the entire ecosystem was ready to go online. 'We founded BigBasket in 2011 and there was no looking back. The business started growing faster and bigger than ever.'

## Surviving and Thriving

Hari claims that a shrunken market with multiple players is 'nothing short of a bloodbath'. He explains that the Indian retail industry is valued at over $1 trillion, with food and grocery comprising 65 percent of this share. He is certain that an industry with a market size of nearly $700 billion cannot be serviced by a single player. In such a scheme of things, he sees competition as a perk. 'When you need to disrupt the existing norms, you need more players to make noise in the market. This will catalyze change and the market will mature faster. The presence of more players in a larger market simply means more traction; it's a win-win scenario.'

It was a smooth run for BigBasket until 2013–14, when a rival funded by two major VCs with deep pockets entered the arena. 'Their business model was completely different from ours and didn't involve any inventory or warehouse; they were an asset-light business. They would pick up orders from the local store and get it delivered. This meant that one had no control over what was available.' In other words, the delivery executive would find out whether the item was available only when they visited the store. Similarly, the quality of the product could be confirmed only in person. Hari adds, 'The quality is especially important when a customer has ordered fresh produce. The fresh produce picked up and delivered would depend on the delivery executive's judgement and his sense of what is best.'

However, since two major VCs were backing them, it prompted introspection within BigBasket's management about the company's future. Hari shares, 'I remember we had serious boardroom discussions to pivot our business model, too. After serious deliberation, we decided to stay put. We knew a grocery business could not be built in this manner and had firm conviction in how we were working. Pivots are important in life and business. When it is necessary, you should take that path and not let your emotions hold you back but don't pivot simply because somebody else is doing it. It was hard to convince the board, but we believed in our model and ourselves, and stuck with it.' Today, BigBasket works closely with 15,000 farmers and delivers more than 3,50,000 orders per day with a team of 25,000 people and a base of 12 million customers.

## Tech and Data in Retail

BigBasket focuses on technology and data to the hilt, so its founder views his firm not as an e-commerce company, but rather as a grocer and retailer solidly powered by technology. 'Technology helps us automate most of our processes and data supplies us with crucial insights and market trends. BB stands sturdy on the shoulders of its marketing team, categorically driven by brand advertising, digital marketing and analytics,' says a proud Hari. BB's in-house data warehouse, according to him, is a critical asset contributing to the firm's success. In fact, BigBasket has a separate team – Brand Intelligence (BI)

– in place that works directly with FMCG companies to give them valuable insights based on real transaction data.

Elaborating on BI's functioning, Hari says, 'Since we have rich consumer data, BI provides actionable insights to the brands associated with us. Getting consumers to fill up questionnaires is not the best way for brands to gauge consumer trends. So we use online channels for more accurate sampling and to further monitor consumer behaviour of the sample set for six months to see whether the observed behaviour has turned into a habit.'

## BB and Its Tributaries

Hari has a proclivity for delving into businesses adjacent to BB, and he beams with parental pride when he describes two such tributaries. 'BB Daily is the channel that delivers fresh produce first thing in the morning. BB Instant is a vending machine in your apartment building that gives you the option to grab basic items at any time of the day or night.' There are a couple of other streams of innovation that BB is exploring at the moment, including beauty products and meat delivery.

## Guiding Light

Although Hari doesn't have and has never had a formal mentor, he looks up to the ones close to him in times of need. 'I admire my father-in-law, Dr E. Sreedharan – the Metro Man of India – for teaching me by example. He has lived his life with utmost discipline and integrity, which has allowed him to be supremely productive. It's pretty simple for him: you stick to a routine, you become more productive.' In Hari's wife, Shanti, who runs a CBSE school with 4,500 students, he sees a unique leader. She is the person he turns to for advice when confronted by a dilemma. Last but not the least, Hari values and feels immensely grateful to his parents, Ambujam Menon and K. P. K. Menon, for the freedom and trust they have always offered him without fail.

## Rejuvenation

Hari enjoys watching cricket and music. As a member of the Karnataka State Cricket Association, he makes it a point to not miss even a single match happening in Bengaluru. 'If I can't watch a match live, you will find me glued to the TV screen,' says an enthused Hari. A singer and deft guitarist himself, he considers music to be a fundamental part of his personal life.

'Last year, my son Varun and I set up a full-fledged music recording studio called The Jam Room, which he now runs. It seems like a fun, commercial venture but my whole objective is to give budding musicians a platform to record their music. I see several people in their twenties working day-time jobs and performing at pubs on the weekends. Most of them don't have any affordable facility to record their own music and practice. When I hang my boots at BigBasket, I'd like to focus completely on The Jam Room and my other passion for supporting vocational education,' says Hari. He hopes to nurture young talent and also make monetary investments in the field of music in the future.

Hari is a family man and enjoys family time whenever he can, despite his busy schedule. He and Shanti are blessed with three sons. At the time of writing, Varun runs The Jam Room, Uttam is a structural engineer in Toronto and Karthik is about to finish his PhD in Fluid Mechanics from Johns Hopkins University, Baltimore.

## Look Before You Leap

Citing his maniacal focus as his biggest asset, Hari shares that he maintains a 'hyper-organized' to-do list and constantly updates it to manage his work efficiently. He endorses a similar well-planned approach when starting something new. Therefore, he recommends startup novices to research the ecosystem before taking the leap. He advises, 'Analyze the ecosystem and make sure it offers an option to scale. Ask yourself if you're too early in the business lifecycle in that ecosystem, or if it already has customers.'

Next comes the funding and in Hari's books, there is no such thing as surplus capital. 'Raise enough capital. People have told me that their stake is more important than excess capital, which, according to me, is foolish. That higher stake has no value if money runs out. If you have a larger amount of money with a lower stake and you are able to scale the business faster, then that lower stake is more valuable than anything else. Simple logic: Raise more money than you need, initially, so that in the long run, you are comfortably placed.'

Hari reiterates building a founding team based on trust. 'Look for trustworthy co-founders, people you have worked or lived with, the ones who understand each other. Don't get emotionally attached, pivot when needed. Do whatever is right for the business, stay on course, and most importantly, believe in yourself.' When hiring, Hari looks for passionate individuals, who reflect relentlessness and display customer empathy. According to him, while the CV could tell you a lot about a candidate's skills, it gives no information about their attitude. The right attitude, Hari insists, is to believe that you may fail, but be confident that you will get right back up, learn from your mistakes, and move forward. 'I give the person a rope, and it's up to him to either use it to climb or tie a noose around his neck.'

## Back to BITS

Since his son Karthik is a BITS Goa alumnus, Hari's connection with BITS remains fresh as ever. 'My parents never visited the Pilani campus, but my wife and I made it a point to visit our son's campus several times. In fact, I chose to receive my Distinguished Alumnus award at the Goa campus.' Hari attributes his entrepreneurial skills to BITS, which prepared him through the right learnings and mindset, to start a successful venture later in his life. The strong BITSian presence in the startup ecosystem is a matter of pride for Hari. 'Entrepreneurship suddenly became visible in the last decade. You see a lot of BITSians in this sphere because of the culture at BITS. Colleges such as IIT Delhi, which are based in a major city, are prone to distractions of the urban life. BITS's isolated location made sure that we bonded with the people around us.'

BITS was also the place where Hari nurtured his love for music. 'I spent a good part of my college life as a member of the Music Club. Practices used to run late into the night. If you go to the room where we used to practise, you can still see "Hari is coming" written on one of the walls because I was always running late,' he reveals with a chuckle.

Hari confidently states, 'BITS is the only Indian university which gives you abundant flexibility and freedom, which is a double-edged sword. You can use it to your advantage, or you can let it destroy you. You can choose to pace your curriculum to your desire – you are assigned a room of your own which gives you time to be yourself and allows you to have your personal space. In most places, you will find that the way things work is predetermined. But at BITS, you structure your life. There is no attendance, so you can choose to break yourself or make yourself.'

# SEEK NEW ADVENTURES

## Harish Bhat, Brand Custodian, Tata Sons

Harish Bhat is the brand custodian at Tata Sons and serves as the chairman of Tata Coffee Ltd. Apart from this, he is also a director on the boards of other Tata companies, including Trent Ltd, Infiniti Retail, Tata Starbucks, Tata Unistore and Tata AIA Life Insurance Company. He joined the Tata Group in 1987 and during his thirty-four-year-long career, he has held several senior roles, such as MD of Tata Global Beverages and COO of Titan. Harish is an alumnus of BITS Pilani and IIM Ahmedabad. He won the IIM Ahmedabad Gold Medal for scholastic excellence in 1987. A decade later, he was awarded the Chevening Scholarship for Young

Managers by the British Government. In 2017, he received the Distinguished Alumnus Award from BITS Pilani. The same year, the Advertising Club and the Advertising Agencies Association of India (AAAI) felicitated him with the Champions of Excellence award, in recognition of the successful brands he had created in partnership with the advertising industry over three decades. Harish was also named in the LinkedIn Top Voices 2019 India list.

While his professional interests lie in brands and marketing, consumer behaviour and business history, Harish is also a prolific writer who contributes regularly to publications such as *Hindu BusinessLine* and *Mint*. He has three books to his credit, including the national bestseller *Tata Log*, which narrates anecdotes from the modern history of the Tata Group. In 2020, he published his first work of fiction, titled *An Extreme Love of Coffee*.

## Business as a Guiding Light: The Tata Group

'WHEN JAMSETJI TATA ESTABLISHED THE TATA GROUP IN 1868, he had the vision of creating a business group where the community was at the centre stage,' says Harish. 'Now, to put that vision into practice, there are many things that he did. Every business venture that he chose to pursue, aimed to do good for the nation. Tata Power was established because he thought clean hydroelectric power would be important for

India. Similarly, steel was very important for the development of our nation's infrastructure. Hence, Tata Steel was founded.'

Jamsetji Tata believed that pioneering ventures that would help the nation advance and flourish should be the group's guiding light, Harish tells us. 'This vision was put into practice by having 66 percent of the shareholding of Tata Sons transferred to the Tata Public Charitable Trusts.' Quite unique, he notes, before continuing, 'Many business groups in the world are majority-owned by promoters, PE funds, the founding families, other business groups and shareholders, but very, very few are majority-owned by public charitable trusts.' It is well known that the majority owners of the Tata Group are the Tata Charitable Trusts, and that is why over the past several decades, 66 percent of all dividends of Tata Sons have been going to their coffers. These funds have been invested in building institutions such as the Tata Cancer Hospital in Mumbai and the Tata Medical Centre in Kolkata – with the intention to serve the most deserving segments of society, says Harish – as well as the Tata Institute of Social Sciences and the Tata Institute of Fundamental Research, which he calls 'progressive institutions which have served India's development'.

'The foremost amongst these institutions, that our founder Jamsetji Tata himself helped establish, was the Indian Institute of Science (IISc) in Bangalore, which many people in the garden city still refer to as the Tata Institute.' Pioneering and serving the community are the two pillars on which the Tata

Group has stood and flourished in the last 150 years, Harish points out cogently. 'I think that the very philosophy of living in harmony with the community is what has made the Tata Group survive and thrive for so long. And that's exactly why so many of us are proud to work with the group. It's really because we know that at the end of the day, the work that we do and a significant portion of the profits that we earn as a very competitive and successful business group, will go back to society, which gives us a very unique sense of purpose.'

## The Journey of a Tata Administrative Services Manager

Harish graduated from BITS Pilani in 1985 and joined the Tata Group as an officer in the Tata Administrative Services (TAS) right after completing his postgraduation from IIM, Ahmedabad in 1987. The journey has been 'a very fulfilling one', says Harish.

'I know that the results of what I am doing, and much of the wealth being generated through my efforts go back to the community and our society. At the same time, the Tata Group has allowed me the opportunity to serve in diverse roles across different industries. These roles have been profoundly interesting, and needless to mention, challenging as well. That has helped me grow significantly, both on the professional and personal fronts.'

At the beginning of his career, Harish worked as an executive assistant to one of the Tata Group leaders,

Mr R. K. Krishna Kumar, who was the then joint managing director of Tata Tea. Soon after, he was made Project Manager in Mr Darbari Seth's office – Seth being the chairman of Tata Chemicals and Tata Tea at the time. The next several years were spent working with the sales and marketing teams of Tata Tea. 'We were competing against Hindustan Unilever (Brooke Bond and Lipton being their well-known tea brands), even as we established our own brands of tea. Back then, we were a rather small brand, just growing into the branded market. So it was fulfilling to take on the giants and win against them. We competed hard and smart, until we became leaders in India's branded tea market.' Following this remarkable line of achievements, Harish was given the assignment of being part of the leadership team that drove the acquisition of Tetley, as a member of the due diligence team. 'This was the first acquisition ever of a global brand by an Indian company and a proud moment for the nation, and for all of us,' Harish recalls.

Then, from the world of marketing and sales of branded tea, the Tata Group transferred him to a new business that was then in the process of being set up as a division of Titan: Tanishq, the now well-known jewellery brand. 'A venture which was back then riddled with financial losses,' reveals Harish. 'We had to fight hard to make it successful. But it was great working under a superb leadership team in Titan, led by marvellous people such as Xerxes Desai, Bhaskar Bhat and Jacob Kurian.' This was followed by a brief stint in the telecom industry and then a long stint as the chief operating officer of Titan – Tata's watch business. 'While Titan as a brand had already been built very successfully, it gave me immense pleasure to further strengthen this brand, and also to participate in the building of a new brand, Fastrack, which became one of the largest brands for Indian youth.' After Titan, Harish served as the CEO and MD of Tata Global Beverages, and he is now with Tata Sons, looking after the Tata brand as its brand custodian.

'So you see,' he says, 'that over the course of the thirty-four years of my career, the Tata Group has given me enormous opportunities in diverse situations and industries, for which I am truly grateful. But in addition to that, the Group has also provided me the space to develop my own passions. I have a strong passion for consumer marketing, creating brands and consumer behaviour, and I feel that the Group has given me a range of assignments to take that passion forward. I'm passionate about writing – an interest that developed during my BITS Pilani days and even prior to that, in school – for which, too, the Group has allowed me enough time and space. In so many ways,' notes Harish, 'the Tata Group has been a brilliant second home to me.'

## The Leadership of JRD Tata

'I was a young manager in the 1980s. Except at an event or two, I never directly interacted with Mr J. R. D. Tata. He was part of my final interview panel at the Tata Administrative Service selections, and I met him briefly at a few subsequent events as well. Although our personal interaction was limited, there's one thing he said which has stuck with me, and which I have actually put up there,' says Harish, pointing to a frame on the windowsill behind him. This frame has been with him in his office for the last twenty-five years at least. It is a quote from J.R.D. Tata: 'We must forever aim for perfection, and never be satisfied with second best, in whatever we do, big or small.' 'That's it. Pretty simple, right?' asks Harish rhetorically. 'But it is extremely challenging to actually put into practice. It requires commitment, rigour and obsession.' That thirst for excellence in whatever we do has stayed with me as one of the prime aspects of J. R. D. Tata's personality. When he was the chairman of Air India (previously Tata Airlines), sometimes he would personally go and check every meal, every seat on the flight and let the airline staff know immediately if something was out of its place. He was a stickler for excellence, which is why within the Tata Group, our apex Award for Business Excellence is called the JRD QV Award, as a tribute to the legendary leader. He also used to lead a group of senior, immensely talented people, such as Mr Nani Palkhivala, Mr Darbari Seth, Mr Sumant Moolgaokar, Mr Russi Mody, amongst others. What appealed to me was how he led them, with a very strong set of purposes and principles, but also with great empathy and adaptability.'

## Cause Marketing

In 2018, we listened to a keynote speech delivered by Harish Bhat at the ad:tech summit at JW Marriott in Mumbai. Among other things, he spoke about the 'Jaago Re' campaign, the popular Tanishq remarriage ad and how the chain store Croma recycles electronic waste. '"Jaago Re" was all about raising civic consciousness,' Harish explains to us now, 'and the Tanishq advertisement advocated for breaking taboos in a certain social space, women's remarriage, which was not generally spoken about in India, at least not back then. Similarly, one of our early Fastrack ads focused on championing the LGBTQ+ community – on celebrating the act of coming out of the closet – and breaking yet another taboo in our society.'

Harish brings us to the present day with the current Croma advertisement campaign which promises to recycle their customers' electronic waste and make sure it is disposed of in the most scientific and sustainable way. 'What it really says is: We are here to take care of it for you,' points out Harish.

'I sincerely believe every brand should have a strong point of view in areas that are relevant to it, and if a brand does good for the people, it will find acceptance in their hearts; it's a win-win scenario. In today's world, consumers like to buy from brands that work for a good cause, that stand for a good cause, and this is predominant particularly in your generation,' he says, pointing to his interviewers, referring to millennial and Gen-Z consumers. 'Corporations *have* to give back to society and there is evidence that many younger consumers today prefer to buy from brands that have their moral compass well aligned. From a business perspective, this is something that will stand brands in good stead in the long run. A purposeful point of view is what will help a brand sail through. Brands have to know what they stand for and also what they will take a stand for.'

## The Evolution of the Average Indian Consumer

Harish observes three significant changes in the nature of the average Indian consumer in recent years. 'I think that consumers today are far more aspirational. They no longer want to put up with shoddy products – that kind of tolerance doesn't exist anymore. There was a time thirty to forty years back when Indians would use products which were suboptimal from a global quality standard perspective, and you'd buy global products only if you travelled abroad. But today, I think consumers want to buy brands of the best quality depending on what's affordable and accessible to them, but nevertheless, the aspiration to always buy world-class products still exists. The second big change is that Indians are willing to spend far more on *experiences* rather than on products and services alone. The propensity of Indian consumers now is to spend *much* more on experiences: movies, travel, adventure, weekend drives out of town, all relatively newer trends that the country is witnessing. The third big change is that the average Indian consumer in the eighties and nineties had a strong mentality of saving. As of today, that inclination has come down significantly. Most consumers want to spend what they earn today on enhancing their present life experience. I think the earlier approach of "let's save everything until we buy our house, or until our child gets married" is changing dramatically.'

## Bombay House

Bombay House is the heritage building that houses the headquarters of the Tata Group. 'All of us who work at Bombay House are truly proud of the building's legacy,' Harish shares fondly. 'But at the same time, we are all very much aware that being in this historic building also places a huge responsibility on our shoulders. When one has worked for a few decades with the Tata Group, there is a strong motivation to leave it at least a little better than when we joined it. Because in more ways than one, the Tata Group is not just a business house, it is an institution that we, as Indians, admire and love.'

He believes that the Tata brand is actually owned by the nation. 'The Tata Charitable Trusts, for example, actually belong to the community, because they are dedicated to the community. Therefore, nurturing this special brand and making sure it is even more cherished in the future is and will always be our top priority.'

## The Chairmanship of Ratan Tata

Almost throughout Harish Bhat's time with the Tata Group, Ratan Tata has been at the helm. 'I am in awe of his grace, his humility, the way he conducts himself, and the way he has led the group,' he readily confesses. 'Above everything else, I salute him for his courage. He had the courage to say, "Let's make India's first car," and that's how Tata Indica was born. He had the courage to say, "As a group, we should consider globalization as one of our key strategic threads going forward." This led to the acquisition of Tetley, Jaguar–Land Rover and Corus. He had the courage to take what was possibly a relatively small group at the time, and give it the size, scale and reach that it has today. He also had the vision to build a powerful and sharp brand identity for the Group. Many of our fundamental systems and processes – be it the Tata Code of Conduct or the Tata Business Excellence Model – the pillars that hold the group together to date, exist because Mr Ratan Tata and his leadership team codified them and put them into place.'

## The Curious Marketer and His Passions

For the first ten or fifteen years of his career, Harish was completely immersed in his work. It was only when he was nearing forty years of age that he once again picked up his passion for writing and quizzing and accelerated his journey into the exciting space of studying consumer behaviour. 'In the first decade of your career, it is crucial to be fully involved in what you do, even if you meander through a few different functional areas. The mantra should be to learn as much as you can, contribute as much as possible, learn, grow, learn, grow. But it doesn't mean you neglect other interests that you have and would like to pursue for the rest of your life. After working for about ten years, I was certain that I had a real affinity for consumer behaviour, marketing and branding. So I started to focus far more on these specific areas. When you find something you are really passionate about, you enjoy doing it time and again. Then it just stops feeling like work and becomes a lifelong passion.

'My book, *The Curious Marketer*, is a product of my curiosity. For instance, when someone gifted me a wonderful bottle of Manuka honey, my mind kept mulling over all the different kinds of honey, what honey can or can't do for you, how it is produced, how differently people can market it, what is its market potential, and so on. In fact, this led to one of the essays in the book. Curiosity leads to a certain interesting line of thinking, and that thinking, in turn, generates new enquiries and new ideas. *The Curious Marketer* brings together about fifty-odd essays on fifty different subjects, all of which are the output of my curiosity. It's important for marketers to be curious because curiosity leads to dramatic improvements in everything that we do; curiosity leads to new products and services; curiosity leads to new ideas that stimulate our minds so beautifully. To be curious, you have to read, ask questions, seek new adventures and experiences.'

## Word to the Wise

Passion and patience are the bedrock of success, according to Harish. 'Find your passion. And then give it everything you have. Even as you are doing so, ask yourself: "How can I give a little bit more to the community and the people around me?" People can become very successful, but it takes time to identify one's true passion – that doesn't happen overnight.

Sometimes, you have to traverse various roads before you find your calling, and it is perfectly fine to wander a little bit before you reach your destination.'

'Passion is a quality I have found in so many BITSians.' Talking about how BITS Pilani is an institution that cultivates passion as well as smart decision-making in its students through everyday activities, he says, 'The campus is so full of interesting activities – you have to choose between them, decide what you wish to do, and then there is so much opportunity to contribute to them. When you frame your own timetable at the start of each semester, you have to make quick decisions. And then, when you have to choose from amongst all these myriad campus activities, you have to make quick decisions there, too. Our complete involvement with our hostels and our campus life made us passionate about whatever we did. That is the essence of life: Finding what you love and doing it with spirit. Pilani teaches us that, in more than full measure.'

## Back to BITS

'BITS Pilani's flagship events, Oasis (the cultural festival) and APOGEE (the technical festival), are very dear to my heart. I still remember the Oasis festival that was organized during my term as the BITS Pilani Students' Union President, but I also fondly remember the Oases from my first three years in college. I think the festival has a unique, partly bohemian, partly intellectual feel to it, which all of us used to thoroughly enjoy.'

As a student, Harish actively participated in various activities on campus. 'I still remember representing BITS at Just-a-Minute (JAM) in some college cultural festivals, including Oasis, in my first year, and conducting quizzes and debates through ELAS, the English Language Activities Society, in my second and third years. In my final year, I remember deciding to contest Students' Union elections, trying very hard to obtain sponsorships from companies for Oasis, and then also drafting the Constitution for the Students' Union. We were also delighted when we got Nitin Mukesh to hold a music concert on campus, on the final day of Oasis. In those days, getting someone of that stature to Pilani, given its remote location and our own limited funds, was a huge challenge and yet, we managed to put up a splendid and memorable event that rocked the auditorium.

'Two important BITS traditions were born during my five years on campus and I was somewhat involved in both. One was APOGEE, and the other was *Camel Post*, our monthly magazine. *Cactus Flower* – the annual magazine – was also born during that time, if I recall correctly,' shares Harish, beaming with pride. 'As for APOGEE, we conceptualized it along with Professors Mandke and Venkateswaran, and under the overall guidance of Dr C. R. Mitra, the director at the time.'

A visit to the campus three years ago reminded him what BITS means to him. 'When I went back to Pilani in 2018 for my daughter's convocation (she studied in BITS Pilani as well), I realized again how truly liberal BITS Pilani is as an institution, as a campus. To my knowledge, it is the only campus in the country where class attendance is not mandated. You do have to eventually clear your exams, but there is so much else happening on campus all the time. And because of its secluded location and distance from cities, it has developed its own beautiful culture. Students here learn to live quite independently. I think BITS Pilani is a wonderful crucible for life. There are very few campuses which are so liberal that they permit you to do whatever you wish to. But, at the end of the day, the responsibility is really yours: framing your timetable, selecting your classes, deciding to attend or not to attend them, making sure you are learning as much as you would like to. I will credit BITS Pilani with a lot of what I have been able to do later in life, for giving me my liberal view of life, and for my passion to pursue what I hold dear to my heart. I am so proud of being a BITSian.'

# PASSION IS CONTAGIOUS

## Mahesh Babu, Former MD and CEO, Mahindra Electric

Mahesh Babu is former Managing Director and Chief Executive Officer of Mahindra Electric, a pioneer of electric mobility in India and a part of the $20.7 billion global federation of companies under the Mahindra brand.

He is a Fulbright Scholar and has completed his Leadership in Management from Tepper School of Business, Carnegie Mellon University, and his postgraduate degree in Engineering from BITS Pilani. Mahesh has been featured in the LinkedIn Power Profiles 2018 in India and was honoured by AsiaOne with the 'India's Greatest CEO' award (2017–18).

Under his leadership, Mahindra Electric launched four new electric vehicles, and a mobility platform, NEMO, which stands for Next-Generation Mobility. He has been instrumental in shaping electric mobility solutions for the future, through pathbreaking initiatives in the commercial fleet segment and by expanding the electric portfolio from 48V to 650V drivetrains.

Mahesh was with the Mahindra Group for over twenty-two years. He worked in design and development of engine and vehicle platforms, from frugal three-wheelers to flagship models. The Mahindra XUV500, India's first monocoque SUV, which won twenty-five auto awards within a year of its launch, is one of the most prestigious projects executed under Mahesh's leadership. He holds two joint patents and has won the Mahindra Group Innovation Award twice, first for the development of the Scorpio SUV turbo-charged engine and then for the development of the premier Indian Common Rail SUV, Scorpio CRDe.

A true automobile enthusiast at heart, driving remains Mahesh's real passion. Next in line is his keen interest in sports, specifically cricket.

## At Mahindra

MAHESH SPENT THE FIRST EIGHT YEARS OF HIS CAREER AS a powertrain engineer working on the Scorpio project, after which he went on to lead the team responsible for manufacturing one of India's most successful SUVs. 'This was an enriching journey for me, to move from one division to the other. Every day is a learning opportunity and even today, after two decades with Mahindra, I cannot assert that I know it all. There's just so much to learn every day, everywhere. I have been entrusted with various projects throughout my career and I feel fortunate to have continued my learning through the years. We recently launched Mahindra Treo in the electric three-wheeler segment.' Mahesh believes that one must continuously speak with their customers in order to keep learning. 'For example, by talking to an auto driver, you will learn something new about the three-wheeler market. Just keep your curiosity alive. I feel youngsters are more curious to learn because they have no baggage.'

Mahesh considers himself fortunate to have had a cross-domain experience and emphatically mentions that it is highly beneficial to be inquisitive and observant while shifting domains. He believes being mindful of every moment makes one a better learner and a master decision-maker.

Mahesh accredits most of his knowledge of management to Anand Mahindra (Chairman, Mahindra Group) and Pawan Kumar Goenka (MD, Mahindra Group), and has constantly felt inspired by such personalities at the helm. 'Anand sets long-term goals and thinks out of the box to achieve them. He thought of electric mobility in 1999, when nobody, not even the executives at Mahindra, were convinced, which is a testament to the fact that his approach is in no way myopic.

'My learning has been tremendous and I'm immensely proud to be associated with Mahindra because the firm gives you the liberty to live your life, to cultivate an identity.'

## First Mover's Advantage

Mahesh beams with pride when he tells us that Mahindra EVs (electric vehicles) have covered 250 million kilometres on Indian roads across all terrains and temperatures. He believes India is a unique market. Since it is a tropical country, the batteries and instruments need to be handled differently, often with more care than in less inclement regions, because the high temperatures are extremely unfavourable.

'Being veterans in the automobile industry and having a diverse range of products – from three-wheelers to buses – gave Mahindra a head start to penetrate the EV market. With five to six EV products already in the market, Mahindra can gauge and analyze their performance and thus, learn faster.'

According to Mahesh, it is important to note the difference between the traditional automobile industry and the EV industry. For the former, construction of complex parts requires a huge capital investment, whereas for EVs, the process is much simpler. 'There is a huge opportunity in self-driving and shared mobility options. Charging station is a whole new market in itself, so is energy storage. Innovation can come in many areas – energy, mobility, transport time – the list goes on.'

## Responsible Growth

Mahesh, along with Mahindra's EV wing, strongly believes that automobiles contributing to pollution should not be part of the legacy being passed on to the next generation. 'I am happy to be in this business where I'm able to contribute a little bit to society,' states Mahesh, going on to describe Mahindra's EVs to be environment-friendly as well as economical. Talking specifically about three-wheelers, he asserts that an electric auto might allow one to earn three or four thousand rupees more than the conventional ones.

Mahesh is convinced that using EVs is the only way forward since the quantity of India's oil imports and the consequent pollution is not environmentally sustainable anymore. 'Subsidies provided by the government have made it conducive for manufacturers and consumers to shift to EVs,' explains Mahesh, referring to the Faster Adoption and Manufacturing of Hybrid and EV (FAME) scheme launched by the Indian government, and a global aim of going carbon neutral by 2050 and carbon positive by 2070.

## EVs: Competition or Collaboration?

When asked about Mercedes, Tesla and Nissan's attempts to dominate the Indian EV markets, Mahesh simply says that Mahindra doesn't see them as competition. 'In fact, when Tata sold their first electric vehicle, Mahindra welcomed it. Anything good for the world should be viewed as collaboration, not competition. When all vehicles on the road become electric, only then does it become competition.'

He feels optimistic about the future of electric mobility, given that there has been significant support from the central and state governments, industries and end users. 'The customer's pain points are evident and so is their desire to live a quality life. When I'm asked what line of work I'm in, my answer isn't "making electric vehicles", but "improving the quality of life".'

## Challenges to the EV industry

'Mind. The first obstacle is always one's mental block – that something cannot be done,' says Mahesh. 'But that obstacle has now been overcome. The government, too, has made it clear that as a nation we need to move towards a cleaner future, which is prominently seen in Niti Aayog's transformative mobility solutions and Mission 2032 indicating when India will be an all-electric nation.'

Mahesh is well aware that an unconventional idea will always be met with resistance but believes that it isn't reason enough not to pursue the idea.

The significant population shift from rural to urban areas has made mass rapid transportation, electric mobility and other transformative transportation methods necessary. 'The average purchasing power has increased, and everyone would like to have a car now. The solution is to roll out more EVs or, better yet, convert private vehicle users into public transport users and provide last-mile connectivity. People's interest first, then the nation's, followed by the industry, then your company and then you,' says Mahesh, placing strong trust in this hierarchy of responsibility.

## The Mahindra Way

About the curious case of naming Mahindra cars – all of them end with an 'o' – Mahesh tells us that there is no rationale behind it. 'It was coincidental. We started with Bolero and it became a hit. Since then it has become a thing. Every brand has some tone in it – one that resonates across the firm. We all love it and would like for it to remain that way. There is no science behind it; it's just a feeling.'

Mahesh further explains that ventures across Mahindra are allowed to grow freely and develop a flavour of their own, and, at the same time, are glued together by Mahindra's core values. 'Mahindra & Mahindra's culture is different from Mahindra Electric, and quite rightly so. While the former is well established, the latter has more flexibility, almost like a startup. But the amount of respect employees have for each other in both ventures is identical. There have been times when projects don't do too well, but there is no fear of failure and no respect lost.'

When asked about what makes Mahindra unique, Mahesh claims with pride, 'Mahindra's towering success is because of its strong moral ground. We might lose business, but not ethics.'

## Road to Becoming CEO

'Passion is contagious,' declares Mahesh, speaking about a value he solemnly swears by. Taking us back to the time when he was a novice moving across departments to find his footing, he shares, 'Early on in my career, I wanted to work in Engine, and then move to Combustion. Instead, I was put into Testing.' His boss immediately sensed that he was upset. Mahesh still remembers his words, 'It's a game of cards; you got dealt a bad set. The only way you get better at this is if you win with whatever you have. What's special about winning with all aces?'

'Enabling the ordinary to achieve the extraordinary is your greatest achievement as a leader,' notes Mahesh, for whom a true leader is someone who can be a source of hope in the most uncertain times. 'A true leader sees hope in ideation and works in the right direction, without actually knowing what the output is going to be. At the beginning of anything new, the probability of success might be zero, but hope and diligence are what take that probability up to 90 percent.'

While giving up is very easy, as Mahesh puts it, with a 'keep trying' attitude and striving to achieve the extraordinary, one can stand their ground in the face of any challenge.

Planning and strategizing with the team, as well as adapting to changes make for a competent leader. 'You can also always correct your course midway. Even if you have decided to do something new, you should have the courage to give it up, learn from it and get back to work the next day. At times, you try your best but nothing happens and that is fine. You will have the gut feeling as a leader to amend your ways. You might try something ten times and end up with no results. Just change your strategy or sit down with your team and plan something else.'

## Smells Like Success

'Being intrinsically motivated has worked wonders for me,' Mahesh is quick to respond when asked about the core values that led him to success. 'You have to be motivated and you have to find that motivation by yourself, within yourself. The quest for extrinsic sources of motivation is bound to end in dejection,' asserts Mahesh, who truly believes flattery diminishes excellence.

'A self-driven individual is markedly more productive, more focused and a better decision-maker.'

## Back to BITS

Mahesh's time at BITS was a unique experience, as he had enrolled in the WILP '97 course offered under the Work Integrated Learning Programme (WILP) at the institute. Initially, he found the system of remote learning novel and tough to manage, as the teaching style was a departure from the traditional classroom setup he had been accustomed to. Distance learning, though the norm during Covid times, was an uncommon concept then. 'We were required to appear for exams in person and all the lectures took place over the weekend at the centres. Once I got the hang of it, the whole concept seemed convenient, and it complemented my work schedule and didn't disrupt it much.'

Mahesh was initially apprehensive about the WILP programme as it wasn't a popular course back then, but the fact that it was offered by BITS Pilani assured him of its credibility. 'Looking back, it was an interesting experience, and the programme lent a significant boost to my professional career.'

# ROLL UP YOUR SLEEVES

## Nandini Chopra, MD, Alvarez & Marsal

Nandini Chopra is a managing director with Alvarez & Marsal Corporate Finance & Restructuring in Mumbai, India. Alvarez & Marsal (A&M) is a New York-headquartered global professional services firm. Nandini has nearly thirty years of experience in mergers and acquisitions, joint venture advisory, financial restructuring, bankruptcies, private equity raises, valuations, IPOs and debt syndication. One of her recent notable deals was the six-billion-dollar sale of Essar Steel in a high-profile bankruptcy proceeding to ArcelorMittal Nippon Steel India.

Nandini began her career in 1993 with SBI Capital Markets, the investment banking arm of India's largest commercial bank, the State Bank of India. For five years at SBI Capital Markets, she worked on large capital market raises, including IPOs and rights issuances, as also debt syndication. Prior to joining A&M in 2014, Nandini spent fifteen years with KPMG India in the Corporate Finance practice, where she led a wide range of deals across sectors, primarily focusing on the consumer goods sector. She also set up and led KPMG's India Valuations practice for over five years till 2013.

Nandini graduated from BITS Pilani in 1991 with a degree in Chemical Engineering and joined XLRI Jamshedpur in 1993 to pursue an MBA.

## Investment Banking

NANDINI, A VETERAN IN THE FINANCE INDUSTRY, BEGAN HER career at SBI Capital Markets. Having spent nearly thirty years in the business, she takes no time to point out how investment banking is a vast field. 'In your early years, be open to working across industries and markets. There's so much to learn. Initially, you might not know what you like. But through the middle overs, you'll want to specialize.' As an engineer, Nandini could always relate better to the manufacturing sector as opposed to services. 'It was tangible – products came out at the end of the assembly line and it was possible to relate to most of them as a consumer would.'

Nandini opines, 'Every industry is unique but finding your way is not a very hard nut to crack if you have a structured approach to understanding the end use, customer base, competitive dynamics and supply chain of the industry of your interest.' With new technologies rapidly replacing old ones, product life cycles (especially in the industrial sector) have become shorter. 'Domains underpinned by critical Indian demographics like consumers, healthcare, financial services and technology sectors, have enjoyed unprecedented growth. Both public markets and private equity money loves these sectors,' says Nandini, joining the dots for us.

'When it comes to markets, experience across diverse markets makes for a well-rounded professional,' remarks Nandini. 'While I have always worked in India, I have done several cross-border deals, either buying companies overseas or selling to overseas buyers. Cultural dynamics, work ethics and different regulatory frameworks add diversity to our work experience.'

## Cross-border Deals

Talking about cross-border deals, Nandini points out that 'target markets for acquisition depend on the growth that underpins the economy'. With an economic growth of nearly 8 percent, markets like India have always made it seem like an attractive prospect to overseas buyers.

To illustrate this point, Nandini takes us back to the time when Coca Cola acquired Thums Up in 1993. 'Since then,

India has been an alluring destination for companies to enter organically or via acquisitions. The real challenge is posed by the high valuations that continue to thrive in India. Buyers take time to get their heads around top-line valuations versus earnings-based valuations that they are used to witnessing in their home markets.'

But the drivers for outbound activity are different according to Nandini. Indian companies have shopped for patents, technology and for better-priced markets for their products, hoping to drive better margins from cheaper sourcing back home.

In the early 2000s, when Indians sought to acquire a company overseas, they were treated circumspectly. 'But the momentum picked up in the mid-2000s when more and more Indian companies began acquiring targets in Southeast Asia, Europe and the US. Over time, sellers, having grown more confident, began knocking the doors of Indian buyers.' The pride in Nandini's voice is evident.

She follows up with a word of advice. 'One must work sagaciously with investment guidelines of the target industry and markets as they vary for different countries.'

Even though India has gradually opened up investments in different sectors over the last two decades, Nandini believes that some of the carelessly planned ones follow patchy policies, which compels investors to find solutions that are tougher to navigate. But overall, there is no doubt in Nandini's mind that 'the liberalization trend has been largely unidirectional and upward'.

## The Average Indian Consumer

'Consumption is driven by disposable income and exposure. In the last twenty-five years, there has been a visible change in the consumption of goods and services, starting with television and cable networks delivering a wider variety of sticky content, grabbing more eyeballs than ever before. This has created opportunities for brand owners to advertise.'

Nandini recalls the trend of the late 1990s, when Indians, especially the ones in the IT sector, travelled extensively, thereby getting significant international exposure. This is what, according to her, helped foreign brands discover a new target market in India, which consequently turned into fierce competition for the well-entrenched domestic brands.

'India was one of the few markets that had nearly 100 percent cell phone coverage. With the explosion of the internet and rapid adoption of smartphones and social media, consumption moved online. Walmart acquired Flipkart in a record $16 billion buyout. Big-ticket investments in internet companies happened frequently, creating serial unicorns, all of which were banking on the vast Indian demographics underpinning demand.'

The savings mentality of the late nineties had given way to the millennials' credo of living in the moment. Nandini astutely states, 'Disposable income went up more than ever before. The younger generations are now increasingly living on credit. Fin-tech companies have been creating disruptive models to provide financing to the bottom of the pyramid.

The credit culture has percolated through all the economic segments, providing a further fillip to consumption,' concludes Nandini.

## The Most Challenging Deal

This is a no-brainer for Nandini Chopra. 'It was the challenging sale of Essar Steel to ArcelorMittal in a $6-billion deal towards the end of 2019, via a relatively new insolvency code introduced in 2017.' As it turns out, the deal had to be run like any other sell-side but needed to be designed within the framework of a new and untested law. The rules of the game changed frequently, and stakeholders were pulled in all sorts of directions. Owing to the ambiguity of the law, there were no clear directives and hence, the stakeholders' course of action changed and their strategies were reshaped. 'We had to run and manage the steel plant while trying to sell it under hostile conditions. We were not dealing with just a few shareholders but a group of over thirty lenders. Driving consensus and decisions in itself was a mammoth task and a number of judicial courts played a significant role in influencing the twists and turns of the proceedings.'

The deal took nearly thirty months to reach its conclusion – it was a landmark transaction that demonstrated how lenders can find the best recoveries for businesses that were impacted by multiple headwinds.

## Demystifying Private Equity

'I enjoy sell-side advisory the most, as there's always a higher chance of success given multiple buyer interests. These are all different facets of investment banking,' Nandini explains, 'where companies either buy or sell or raise money for growth.' Corporates need advisors to help them navigate with preparation, strategy, valuations, diligence and negotiations. According to her, the hardest part is the contingent nature of the business. 'Despite best efforts, deals can fall through for numerous reasons beyond one's control. You have to learn to live with uncertainty and frustration. But it's worth its weight in gold when you do get a deal across the finishing line.'

## Stress and Rejuvenation

Even though the stakes are undoubtedly high, finance is not the only bastion of stress and burnouts. Nandini believes that professions like medicine or law have similarly high stakes, if not higher. Academia and research are no less challenging.

'Deconstruct the real nature of your deadlines and the cause for one's stress, for many are self-imposed,' she says. 'Most of our stress comes from endless multi-tasking, from being constantly online, which is almost like being in a rat race that you cannot even see. Develop the ability to step out of your role and be a fly on the wall. Watch what's going on.'

Stress is an internal reaction, believes Nandini, and it is up to our individual ability to deal with it. In her own words,

'Prioritize what's important and don't work all year-round for that one big annual vacation. Take time out for yourself every day, many times in the day. Enjoy music while you drive between meetings, read a book every night, learn to play an instrument, write, paint, doodle, play with your children, make time for your parents and give back to your community. Most importantly, enjoy the profession you choose, as you will spend a lion's share of your waking hours at work. Revisit often the reasons you chose to do what you do and try to understand what keeps you motivated.'

## Women in the Workplace

Nandini counts herself fortunate enough to have never felt any gender-based pressure or prejudices. She believes that India isn't really different from any other society, perhaps just a generation behind in terms of accepting that both partners in a marriage must have an active career. 'This is fast-changing,' she points out. 'The choices to continue with one's career or take a break is entirely up to the individual. Indian society values education highly and I see no reason why the same family that educated their daughter and son equally should have a different set of expectations from their daughters and daughters-in-law later on.'

'I have been lucky to have had parents who encouraged me relentlessly to pursue higher education and a career, and to find a life partner for whom my own identity would be a matter of pride. My husband and his family have never questioned my decisions or put me in a position where I had to make difficult choices. My children, too, are extremely proud of my achievements and have never felt that I should have stayed at home for them.'

Nandini gives due credit to her employers as well – 'SBI Capital Markets, KPMG and now Alvarez & Marsal have always supported me through my daily challenges of balancing work and home.' She believes that corporates have come a long way when it comes to facilitating work-life balance for women in the workplace.

## Success Recipe

According to Nandini, the key success factors are tenacity and dogged determination, building a solid foundation in the early years across a wide range of projects, and networking. She is optimistic about the range of corporate opportunities available in the contemporary market. To quote a few examples: straddling corporate and retail banking, investment banking, private equity, stock market investments and trading, wealth management, credit rating, finance functions in corporates – all offer incredible potential.

'If you're lucky, you may be exposed to a few of them before you decide to settle into a specialization. Never underestimate the power of your school and college networks. Always stay in touch and widen your horizons. There's a place for everyone in the system and like you, everyone else also has their own achievements. Never stop learning. Read, read and read. And last but not least, treat everyone with respect always for you are sure to cross paths with someone you had a run-in with earlier.'

One must not underestimate the value of hard work either, says Nandini. 'Spend time. Burn the midnight oil. Roll up your sleeves. Learn the ropes, for there is nothing more valuable than hands-on experience. Never ever seek privileges. Leave your class, community, financial background, religion and gender behind, when you enter the workforce. They are meaningless labels and can act as fetters. Integrity and merit are the only values that matter.'

## Back to BITS

'In 1991, there was the great Indian exodus to the US for pursuing master's and PhD programmes. The ones who couldn't make it would strive for an MBA from the IIMs. We had just emerged from the Mandal Commission protests, a period when students had immolated themselves in their universities to fight against quotas,' Nandini tells us, recalling the tumultuous days when the nation was rocked by students protests. It was around the same time that she was graduating from BITS. The chaos unfurled all over Delhi, not too far from Pilani. Even though everyone in Pilani heard and read about the protests, they couldn't relate to it entirely, the experience never became a first-hand one.

'Admissions to BITS were handed out purely on merit, through a standardized procedure, and hence, we had the good fortune of not being impacted by labels and quotas of any kind.' Summing up her college experience, she says, 'The most unique thing about BITS Pilani is that it treats everyone equally, right from admissions till convocation.' This lesson in equality is something that has guided her throughout what has been an exceptional professional career.

# TAKE UP THE CHALLENGE

## Nilesh Kothari, Co-founder and Managing Partner, Trifecta Capital

Nilesh Kothari is the co-founder of Trifecta Capital which is a new-age platform for startups that provides alternate capital and solutions across three verticals – venture debt, financial tech solutions and equity. The firm boasts of supporting the highest number of privately held startups in the country – nine unicorns and eleven soonicorns. Its portfolio companies include BigBasket, Pharmeasy, Cars24, Vedantu, Infra.Market, ShareChat, Dailyhunt, UrbanCompany, CureFit, CarDekho, Blackbuck, Ninjacart, NoBroker and BharatPe, amongst several others.

Previously, Nilesh served as the global MD (Ventures & Acquisitions) at Accenture. He has also worked with large, reputed Indian conglomerates like the Aditya Birla Group, Hero Group and JM Financial, and was the founding team member at Zenta (successfully exited to Accenture). Overall, he has over thirty years of experience in various finance and business development roles. He has travelled and worked across the world and enjoys working in entrepreneurial, high-growth, diverse and multicultural environments.

Nilesh graduated with a postgraduate degree in Management Studies from BITS Pilani in 1990, where he was an active member of the photography club and the team behind SandPaper – the college's student-run newsletter.

## Trifecta Capital's Perfect-A Portfolio

TRIFECTA CAPITAL IS INDIA'S LEADING ALTERNATE CAPITAL provider which focuses on solving capital gaps in the country, the world's third largest startup ecosystem. Trifecta pioneered venture debt funds in 2015 and is set to launch its third fund. 'Recently, we launched a late-stage equity fund – another first in India – with the objective of providing secondary exit to early investors and employees in startups and growth capital in the US$15–30 million range. We have an incredible portfolio and are proud to have supported founders with alternate capital that is non-dilutive, as well as aided them on different aspects of their business.'

Nilesh proudly shares, 'Trifecta Capital pioneered venture debt funds in India in 2015 and today, stands as the largest, having supplied over US$270 million of venture debt to more than seventy startups. We are constantly innovating and have specialized venture debt products for acquisitions, seasonal working capital requirements and SaaS companies. In the west, thirty-five years ago, traditional banks like Citi, Bank of America and Wells Fargo had neither the expertise nor the regulatory freedom to provide credit to startups. So, new institutions like the Silicon Valley Bank, TriplePoint and Western Technology Investment (WTI) were built and became fairly large and successful. Trifecta was inspired by them.'

The name 'Trifecta' was chosen with care, as Nilesh explains, 'Trifecta is a technical word when one predicts the first three positions in a horse race. It means three winners or a big win. In the context of Trifecta Capital, it means when the founder(s), the VCs and Trifecta come together, they make a winning team!'

## Venture Debt and Limited Partners

Nilesh, along with Rahul (one of India's seniormost venture capitalists), has mentored several startups. It was during Nilesh's stint at Accenture that he met Rahul again after several years. Both of them had always wanted to do something in this space – to create an impact in the startup ecosystem. Both came from high-profile, well-paying jobs and had explored a multitude of opportunities in the startup ecosystem. 'The idea of building an institution that was focused on providing alternate capital and solutions to startups was very appealing. Trifecta is not just a "fund management house" or just a "venture debt fund". It's a platform that is continuously trying to understand the gaps and needs of startups and innovating new products and services,' elucidates Nilesh, who claims that this journey hasn't been easy but 'satisfying and fun' nonetheless. He goes on to add that venture debt has use cases in financing working capital, capex and acquisitions.

'Our goal was to build an institution, to have access to long-term capital pools, to amalgamate the traditional with the new.' This quest for capital led Nilesh and Rahul to 'great institution builders' – the likes of Uday Kotak, Deepak Parekh, Arundhati Bhattacharya and Vishwavir Ahuja. He recounts how difficult the first few minutes of conversations with these pioneers of great financial institutions of the country were, and how much he dreaded being asked a recurring question: 'Why would you lend capital to a startup?' But they eventually came to appreciate the idea and helped build Trifecta.

Speaking about Trifecta's limited partners (LPs), Nilesh proudly calls them 'business partners'. 'Our LPs comprising fifty of the top hundred Indian institutions, and business houses offer immeasurable support to the startups by not only providing capital but also contributing significantly with their expertise and knowledge.'

## Equity Costlier than Debt?

'No business in this world is built only on equity, it's always a combination of equity and debt. The debt depends on factors like cash flows, gestation period and profitability, but debt gives you the flexibility to manage your capital needs – take it when you need it – while an issuance of equity is usually irreversible,' explains Nilesh meticulously. 'The cost of capital is 30 percent for equity in the venture capital world, while "venture debt" is around 10 percent on a post-tax basis. So, factors like cost of capital, return on equity and all such metrics look better when you have debt in your capital structure. It brings down the overall weighted cost of capital and thus helps all shareholders.' Nilesh feels that the biggest issue with equity is that it is expensive, and since most founders build their businesses only via equity, they continue to get diluted. 'The long-term value that they are creating is not from the salary that they draw from the businesses, but the equity they hold in their companies, and if one gives up equity, they're giving up the opportunity to share in the value that they helped create.'

To Nilesh, this is a 'perverse incentive', because if a founder holding equity goes below 10 percent, they might not be so motivated by the time they reach Series E or F of funding. He claims that too little equity for founders is equally dangerous for investors as it's hard to 'import founders'. 'You cannot simply bring in a CEO and say, "You are now a founder". So, venture debt allows that alignment of interest. Giving up too much equity too early on is the biggest regret of all founders in Trifecta's portfolio.'

## Preferred Sector to Invest

Trifecta's goal is to build a diverse portfolio and their investments testify the same. The company has invested across consumer products, healthcare, e-commerce, and in several other sectors as well. 'So, if one company gets impacted because of regulatory reasons, the portfolio is not impacted. We believe in solving India's contemporary problems. There are problems in education, healthcare, logistics, finance and agriculture, and most of them concern rural India and lower-tier (II, III and IV) cities. We believe the next wave of unicorns will be built to solve problems faced by these sectors.'

'We are also collaborating with a couple of venture debt funds and participating in rounds together. In banking, too, there is a concept of consortium banking (multiple banks funding one particular project) and there is no reason why debt providers should not be working together. It helps in diversification, brings together the strengths of multiple organizations and helps a startup raise larger capital.'

## Frugality in Startups

Nilesh believes startups being frugal or not is a grey area and refrains from generalizing the trend. 'Every few years, you see a lot more maturity in the ecosystem. Since the startup ecosystem itself is only fifteen years old, the VCs, investors, founders, everyone is learning.'

The first wave of repeat founders – Mukesh Bansal, Sachin Bansal, Binny Bansal, Vishal Gondal, Hari Menon – makes Nilesh feel hopeful about the stability of this industry's future. 'These are founders who have gained a lot of experience, have learnt from their mistakes and, hopefully, won't repeat them. On the one hand, there are founders who are frugal and cautious about valuation and spending, and on the other, there are a few who are not so careful. At Trifecta, we have seen some very exciting business models and mature founders, and the investor ecosystem in general is also getting smarter, which gets me excited about the future.'

## Foundation Stones

When it comes to the ideal founder, Nilesh believes there needs to be a precise balance between energy and experience. 'I love to work with founders who have some prior experience. I would say the thirty or so age group is the sweet spot.' Nilesh prefers co-founders as opposed to a single founder. 'It is a long, rocky journey, with a fair share of ups and downs. One needs to have co-founders with complementary skills and similar values as one builds an organisation. A good combination goes a long way.'

Asserting the importance of guidance, Nilesh insists that a founder, even an extremely competent one, requires guidance and coaching after the organization reaches a certain scale. 'A great founder is one who realizes when to seek help and from whom to seek it. Founders should learn from other founders, respect their investors, and be willing to have a frank and honest conversation.'

## Career after BITS

Nilesh feels fortunate to have received an array of opportunities after graduating from BITS. 'I took my chances and enjoyed working in startups. When I was with the Aditya Birla Group, I had the opportunity to pick any of the units to work for. I chose to work with the Mangalore Refinery, because it was a new project and the largest in the private sector. I met Nimesh Kampani during my time there and mentioned to him that I wanted to get into financial services.'

Nilesh's career shifted tracks when Nimesh offered him a job in the mutual funds business that the latter was founding – JM Mutual Fund. 'Mutual fund was a sunrise industry at that time, and it seemed like a great opportunity. I ended up working there for about four years. The MF industry is huge, with valuations near 30 lakh crore. I like to take up those kinds of challenges. That is just my personality. I would have struggled in large, stable organisations like Unilever and Procter & Gamble, at the start of my career.' Nilesh's hands-on approach in life makes him look forward to exciting opportunities in and the challenges of new industries.

## Building a Career in Finance

Nilesh's penchant for finance led him to reject a sales role with HCL, a job offered to him during on-campus placements. He complemented his education with a degree in Cost and Management Accounting, which is 'one of the best things' he did for his career. 'I always took up new assignments every few years, even within the same organisation, as I used to get bored of doing the same thing over and over again. And therefore, I have handled several interesting assignments in my life, within finance, including Trifecta Capital, which is something very different.'

Working in business development for several years helped Nilesh bag the 'interesting' opportunity of managing the daunting, long balance sheet at Accenture. 'It was a global role, a big balance sheet to invest from and many exciting deals.'

Nilesh strongly advises a career in finance only if it's an area of interest and emphasizes the importance of reskilling oneself every few years. 'Markets, technology, products – everything is changing and one has to keep up'. Nilesh attributes his entrepreneurial abilities to his training under great leaders like Aditya Birla, Nimesh Kampani and Brijmohan Lall Munjal. He truly believes a role should be taken up only if it is coherent with one's personality. 'Your aptitude, experiences and interactions make life exciting.'

## Play the Long Game

Nilesh affirms that his early exposure to the world of finance worked in his favour. While at Mangalore Refinery, he was a member of the core finance team, which meant he was involved not only in fundraising and project finance, but also building large projects. He emphasizes that a keen sense of observation and proactive approach can go a long way. 'I never restricted myself to just my key result areas (KRAs), my roles and responsibilities, and was always keen to get involved in cross-functional stuff.'

'Invest time in an organisation, and observe your leaders,' Nilesh is quick to remark. He believes the contemporary workforce is constantly switching jobs, which is detrimental to them and the organization. 'See a few seasons, see a few cycles, because that is how you learn. Go through a recession. I think learning is slow when you change organizations. It takes nearly six months to understand what this organization is doing, to start understanding, "*Acha yeh mera role hai*" (Okay, so this is what my role entails). Then one year later, you are moving out. I think people should invest time. If you are getting into a good organization, invest some time there. Because every organization can help you learn. Take the last five years as an example – demonetization, GST, NBFC crisis, war and finally, a pandemic. All these are unique situations. If you spend time through these, there is so much to learn.'

## Back to BITS

Nilesh believes he speaks for most of his batchmates when he says, 'We wanted to get out of Pilani as soon as possible. But when we did, we had a better appreciation for BITS and the rich campus life that it had offered.'

'There were no phones, laptops and only one TV in the common room, on which everyone enjoyed watching *Chitrahaar*. We ate what was served in the mess or went hungry. We didn't have the All-Night Canteen (ANC) back then, but we loved to indulge in the occasional Maggi at the *redis* or at Nutan. Most of us didn't have any money to splurge,' recalls Nilesh. He continues in a reminiscent tone, 'The best thing about BITS was that, since it was a closed campus, everybody knew everybody.'

Ragging, although light and all in good humour, was rampant during his time at BITS. Nilesh chuckles when he says, 'I was ragged too, and that's how we made some very close friends. We used to visit Jal-T a lot.' Looking at our puzzled faces, Nilesh explains, 'Jal Tarang was a Haryana Tourism rest house, twenty-three kilometres away from the campus, in Loharu, which we used to throng to when we had a birthday to celebrate, or sometimes just to have paneer or kali dal. Now, you can go to the ANC.'

Walking down the memory lane, Nilesh recalls all BITSians being extremely enthused about movie screenings in the auditorium back then. 'The last time I was in Pilani, I went to the audi to watch this fantastic movie, but there were only four people, because apparently, everyone had already seen it online on their laptops.'

Nilesh's remains highly appreciative of the holistic life offered at BITS. He credits his alma mater with inculcating a myriad of soft skills in him. 'As a community, BITSians generally do well and have reached leadership positions across all spheres of life. I feel kids entering BITS today are better informed, more ambitious and know what to do next,' says Nilesh in an optimistic tone.

# KEEP AN OPEN MIND

## Phanindra Sama, Co-founder, redBus

Phanindra Sama served as the chief innovation officer for the Government of Telangana from 2017 to 2020. He co-founded redBus.in, India's largest bus ticketing company, in 2006. Phani was ranked third amongst India's Most Promising Entrepreneurs of 2012 by *Business World*. He has been chosen as a young global leader by the World Economic Forum. In 2013, he was awarded Entrepreneur of the Year Award by ET Now. In the same year, he was ranked fourth in the Impact Digital Power 100 list among India's other digital pioneers. He was featured in the 'Fortune 40 under 40' list twice – in 2014 and 2015 – and the 'BITSAA 30 under 30' list in 2012. A Chevening

Fellow, Phani became the second Indian to join Endeavor, a non-profit organization of high-impact entrepreneurs, in 2009.

## Boarding redBus

PHANINDRA, BETTER KNOWN AS PHANI AMONG HIS PEERS, candidly admits that he feels he got lucky with redBus. 'We just happened to start at the right time and the right place. Getting both right is crucial. We didn't know anything about entrepreneurship, it wasn't even a buzzword back then.'

It was a different world. 'YouTube and Facebook had just started. There were no smartphones. There was no internet on the go, hardly anyone had internet in their house. It was a facility available in select offices. With respect to payment gateways, there were only CCAvenues. For every venture capitalist who has invested in us, we were amongst the first batch investees of their first fund.'

## Back to the Beginning

'It all started when we missed a bus,' explained Phani reminiscently. 'We did not know anything about entrepreneurship, we just wanted to solve a simple problem by creating an open-source, free software for bus operators. Once the operators start using that software, all of us would benefit and that was the whole idea. It wasn't really about starting a company. That sort of just happened.'

He reiterates the importance of being in the right place at the right time. Had redBus started two years later, when the internet was just arriving on the scene and credit cards were being used for payment, it wouldn't have been in the game.

Phani also emphasizes the importance of first mover's advantage. The bus operators had asked them not to waste their time. Online booking made sense for airlines, not buses: the clientele was different.

'*Bus me nahi hoga yeh; chalo jaao.*' (This won't happen in the bus business; now go.)

Then there were others, the ones who warned them about getting involved in the bus business. Mainly because it was run by rowdies, *gunda*s, the private industry and the mafia, so to say.

'We didn't have anything to lose, as we were building a free and open-source solution, so we didn't pay much heed to that advice and kept at it. After you take a few steps into the water, you get to know how deep it is, and then you either keep walking in or get right out, but you do that only after being better informed.'

## Launching Your Startup

Phani's association with the Indian startup ecosystem goes a long way back. From his wealth of experience, he shares some tips for budding entrepreneurs.

'Actually, we had worked in large companies for a couple of years before the startup. I think it was beneficial for us, putting that time in, because it's not about at what age you start a company – whether you start at 22, 25, 30 or even 50, it doesn't matter. It's about how big an impact you're making, how successful the company is going to be and all that.'

Phani believes job experience before venturing into the startup ecosystem is invaluable. When redBus was starting out, they had reached out to a college *batchie* (batchmate), who had started his firm fresh out of college.

'When I went to his office, I noticed almost 25 percent of the office space was his cabin, 20 percent was the cafeteria and all the employees were cramped into the remaining space. He also had a peon at his service, and this was more of a traditional way of running a business. This came as a surprise to me since the culture where I then worked – Texas Instruments – was completely different. Everyone, be it a new hire, the manager, or even the country head, worked in the same space. Unlike traditional offices, modern MNCs have no big cubicles, no peons. Everybody is treated equally, it's a flat organization.'

Phani feels working for two years before starting up certainly worked to his advantage. He was able to pick up numerous tricks of the trade. 'We got to know how a performance appraisal is done, how a manager is supposed to treat his or her employees. We learnt important soft skills: why salary shouldn't be discussed with other people; how office politics work, among other things.' By putting in the time and effort, he gained insight into the work dynamics of a business.

'Having gone through it and benefited from it, I would say it is great to have that experience, but at the same time, if you have a great idea, you might miss out if you don't act on it.'

## Role of a Mentor

Acknowledging the significance of finding good mentors, Phani remembers how his mentors had advised him to keep at it. It was at this point that redBus switched from being a startup to being a firm in its own right. Today, it continues to be a flourishing business, operating in six countries across the world.

According to Phani, a mentor's impact stretches beyond the realm of the mentee's career. 'It made all the difference to us. The things that I talk about today are all drawn from advice given by our mentor.'

'The difference between a mentor and a consultant is that with a mentor there is continuity. He has known you over a long period of time. You don't have to go and tell him the background story for every piece of advice. The best way to choose a mentor is to choose a person who has done it all. Someone who has been an entrepreneur, who has gone through it all. It need not be in your field. But he should gel well with your personality. I am not aggressive, so I needed somebody to match my pace,' shares Phani.

But he cautions that a mentor must be chosen with care. 'When you have a conversation with so many people, you just click with some of them. I signed up a mentor who was immensely successful, had a large company employing maybe lakhs of people, and he was a self-made entrepreneur. I respected him, he also liked me but he never had time. We hardly met. Once, I went to his office to ask for help but he was very busy and connected me to his CEO. But I wasn't seeking help from his CEO. Even now when we meet somewhere, we discuss things, but that is not enough. Mentoring means setting aside some time to meet and talk every week. So, a mentor is also the person who has time dedicated just to you.'

## Ethics in Business

When it comes to competitors who have more money, Phani asserts, it is the company culture, people, capabilities and talent you cultivate that come in handy. 'Every now and then, there is stress in our company, so our team would say things like "Oh my God, the competitor launched some big discount, like a-rupee-a-ticket from anywhere to anywhere in India". They came up with hoardings, with newspaper ads and all of our team was shit scared.' For a moment, everyone feels that redBus is doomed to never see the light of day again.

'Once, a company was threatening our existence, which worried the team a lot. This was a firm that would go to any extent; they had got some RTCs – road transport corporations – on board, including government RTCs, through bribery. We didn't have RTCs for a long time because we waited until they would come to us without being bribed. RTCs were synonymous with a voluminous inventory simply because they would have 7,000 to 8,000 buses. RTC bus fares are also a little lower than that of private buses and there is more trust because it is a government driver.'

At that point, Phani simply asked his team, 'How many of you would like to go and work for that company?'

'Nobody wanted to, because for those highly talented, self-respecting individuals, working for a cause and being ethical was of utmost importance. Let's say you are graduating from BITS and have two choices in front of you. Your first option is a startup that doesn't object to bribery and is ready to use any means to maximize profits, and the second option is an equally competent startup that may sometimes lose out on the profits, but never compromises on its ethics. Which company would you join?' asks Phani rhetorically.

Phani is guided by a strong sense of business ethics. 'Firms like Tata, Wipro have shown the country that a company can become wildly successful, yet remain ethical, which is how I want redBus to always be,' says Phani passionately. 'If you trust in your team's calibre, you needn't worry if your competitor comes up with fancy schemes by using unethical measures. If your firm's moral fibre is intact, your employees would never join an unethical competitor.'

He believes the industry is filled with such examples. 'Azim Premji – one of the richest Indians – has achieved immeasurable success without once sacrificing his ethics and values.' Phani's mentors used to share numerous anecdotes of Azim Premji with him.

## Success Mantra

'Keep an open mind. Attract good talent. Retain them.' Phani's business philosophy is based on his belief in the power of a knowledge economy and how attracting good talent is the primary key to success.

He believes that while the nature of today's knowledge economy is hyper-competitive, a firm can thrive if it hires competent employees, makes them feel empowered and retains them. 'Almost all the senior management we hire, have spent at least five years in one of their previous companies. I also experimented and hired people who had jumped jobs every two years, but it wasn't useful. If I have to enable them to be their best, I should let them make decisions. I always tell myself, "I'll decide who gets into the bus, but not where the bus goes." If you want people to stick with you, that is the kind of freedom you must give them. The longer the more capable people are with you, the fewer the setbacks for the company.'

Phani states, 'It's not the funding. After a point, it's most definitely the talent that makes a firm big.'

## Back to BITS

Phani graduated from BITS Pilani back in 2002. As we exchange notes, Phani remarks how a lot has changed since then. 'I saw pictures where the sprawling garden in front of the iconic clock tower – C-lawns, as we used to call – had been replaced by the beautiful New Academic Block (NAB),' says Phani admiring the new architecture, albeit with a hint of sadness for the 'diminishing greenery'.

With a substantial increase in the number of admissions, there has been a proportional increase in hostel capacity. The previously H-shaped hostels, or 'bhawans', as they are called in BITS, with the addition of new wings have metamorphosed into digital 8-shaped structures. It looks more like a concrete jungle now. There are grills around the hostels now,' laments Phani, but the news of no 11:00 p.m. curfew for girls – which allows them to participate in co-scholastic activities hassle-free – was a pleasant surprise for him.

He agrees that the campus is moving in the right direction with new facilities such as a bigger library and campus-wide internet access. In his time, computers were just coming in. But that did not stop people from making the most of the resources they had. One of his classmates – one of the few who owned a computer – used to create applications for fun as side projects.

'He was really passionate about coding and used to do it all the time. He used to create all sorts of applications and plug them in. Just as you entered his room, his speakers would start – for lack of a better word – speaking.

'We obviously didn't have the internet and worked on a standalone computer. We didn't even have a graphical user interface (GUI) back then. GUIs came into the picture after we had graduated from college, and around the same time, Google search became prominent as well. There was an application called Pine. Just like MS-DOS, to write mails you execute a command and then it opens a compose window, which is basically a new terminal where you can compose the mail.'

'We could have really used an entrepreneurship cell back then,' says Phani with a slight chuckle.

# COMPASSION, LOVE AND EMPATHY

## Pradeep Kashyap, Founder, MART

Pradeep Kashyap worked with MNCs for seventeen years before starting MART as a 'Business Mind Social Heart' consultancy organization. Currently, he is also a consultant for the World Bank and the United Nations. He has been a marketing advisor to the Ministry of Rural Development and has served as a member of the Prime Minister's Office, several chief minister committees on rural development, advisory committees of the Reserve Bank of India and the National Bank for Agriculture and Rural Development.

Pradeep also spearheaded the globally acclaimed Project Shakti with Hindustan Unilever to appoint 60,000 poor women as dealers for the company. He has pioneered many sustainable business and marketing models, including inclusive marketing, public-private-community partnerships and last-mile distribution models with Colgate, Tata Steel, Novartis and others. He has helped generate additional income for 200,000 poor women by ensuring their produce reached bigger markets. He is a recipient of the Jamnalal Bajaj Award for Outstanding Contribution to Rural Development (1991). He was also awarded the Lifetime Achievement Award by Rural Marketing Association of India in 2013 and the Distinguished Alumnus Award by BITS Pilani in 2014. The title of the 'Father of Rural India' by late Professor C. K. Prahalad was bestowed upon him for his immense contributions to rural development in India.

## Journey to MART

PRADEEP JOINED EXIDE, A MULTINATIONAL COMPANY IN Calcutta, after graduating from BITS in 1969. After spending seven years at Exide, he spent another seven at MICO-Bosch, before finally joining Denso – the world's largest auto ancillary – as the head of marketing. 'I worked in these three MNCs for seventeen years with reasonable success. But I was getting increasingly restless as I did not want to continue in the corporate world for the rest of my working life. I was fortunate that around this time, I met my spiritual guru – Sri Madhav Ashish (a Padma Shri awardee), an Englishman and aeronautical engineer who came to India during the Second World War to repair Spitfire engines, never to return to his country of birth.'

Pradeep met his guru in 1980, when he was running an ashram, a few kilometres away from Almora. It was Pradeep's guru who encouraged him to enquire into the purpose of life. 'The year I turned forty, I decided with the blessings of my guru that I should change the course of my life. I voluntarily opted out of the corporate sector to serve the poor,' says Pradeep, with immense satisfaction.

He feels fortunate to have been appointed as the marketing advisor to the Ministry of Rural Development, a role which gave him the opportunity to travel pan-India and witness rural poverty at the grassroots. 'I realized I had to do something about it. I decided to start a professional organisation to help create large-scale livelihoods for the poor. But having experienced the impersonal "what's in it for me" culture of multinationals, I was determined that my organisation would cultivate a strong sense of belonging and self-sacrifice among its employees. MART was established in 1993 supported by the pillars of family values of transparency, belongingness and caring, with the CEO as the head of this family.'

The pride in Pradeep's voice is palpable when he tells us that most of the team members have been with MART for about two decades. 'In today's world, that is very rare, and this is all because we are a family, and we believe no one leaves their family. Professor Ishwar Dayal – the first director of IIM Lucknow and the doyen of management education – wrote a business case study on the family-oriented organizational structure at MART when he was ninety!'

## Pillars of MART

Pradeep believes a CEO's fundamental role is to motivate the team by engaging with their emotions. 'The key to their hearts is a story,' says Pradeep, who has a knack of sharing stories at staff birthdays, weddings and weekly meetings.

'When I turned sixty in 2007, I decided to pass on the legacy. I inducted four seniormost professionals at MART as partners and gave them a significant shareholding in the establishment. By 2012, the number of partners had doubled.' A secret ballot to choose the next CEO was conducted, and Pradeep personally groomed the chosen person. 'Leadership is your belief system – it cannot be taught. If your attitude is right, if you are a genuine and compassionate human, then you are a natural leader,' claims a sagacious Pradeep.

For Pradeep, learning is a never-ending process. He advises to always surround oneself with individuals more knowledgeable than oneself. At MART, constant learning is a significant part of the company culture. Pradeep explains this with an analogy from Physics, 'I tell my team to carry an imaginary pipe with them, and connect it to anyone more knowledgeable than them. By the law of gravity, just like water flows from a full tank to an empty tank at a lower height, knowledge will flow into them effortlessly, provided they consider their tank to be empty.'

'I worked in the auto sector throughout my career. I didn't know anything about branding, marketing or segmentation. I had never visited a village before moving to the social work sector. Yet I went on to author a book on rural marketing which is prescribed at most IIMs and other prestigious management institutes today,' says Pradeep, attributing his success to his unquenchable curiosity.

## Challenges

While travelling the country, Pradeep came across *haats* (weekly markets) in a lot of villages. 'The villagers told me, "*Yahan pe local maal milta hain.* (You get the local products here)." I came back to Delhi and quizzed the officials in the ministry about these haats. Most of them didn't have any knowledge on the subject and dismissed haats as being of no importance to rural development.'

Pradeep had seen huge haats by then, some that accommodated up to 800 stalls. 'I approached the Additional Secretary of the Ministry of Rural Development in Delhi and convinced him to fund a study of haats. That's when I put together a team and started MART.' The study found that haats are responsible for 25 percent of all the consumption in rural India. Haats are the nerve centre of sociocultural and economic rural life where producers get an opportunity to interact directly with the consumers. 'These producers had no access to markets elsewhere. There are 42,000 haats in India which provide a ready marketing platform,' explains Pradeep, while commenting on the potential of these rural markets.

With the Rural Infrastructure Development Fund, a new NABARD scheme to fund panchayats for improving the infrastructure at haats and many companies using haats to promote their products, the interest in the future of these haats has grown exponentially to an extent that information pertaining to them is now collected by Census of India, as a result of their study.

'If your search for knowledge is sincere, you can change the way national institutions think and influence policy,' concludes Pradeep.

## Project Shakti

In 1998, Pradeep and MART were working with the Andhra Pradesh government to support livelihood opportunities for a group of women in the state. He noted that there was a high possibility of business losses, since most of these women sold vegetables, fish and other perishable items. That's when he conceived the idea to help them shift to selling corporate goods like sugar, salt, tea and soap, which are consumed by the majority of rural homes. It equipped rural women with basic skills that small-scale entrepreneurs need.

These women learn various aspects of running a retail business and this paves the path for the women to become financially independent and more empowered.

'I presented the idea of these women selling corporate products door-to-door in their village. Fortunately, *Economic Times* reported on this idea and two years later, it was also mentioned in a report McKinsey did for HUL. I approached the HUL director with the newspaper cutting. He was convinced of our capabilities and signed MART as the national implementation partner for the rollout of Project Shakti.' His friends and acquaintances from the development sector warned Pradeep that he was wasting his time. They thought that it would distract him from the other innovative projects he was working on at the time. Though a little apprehensive about the project, he gracefully replied with, 'Nothing ventured, nothing gained.'

'As they say, the rest is history,' says Pradeep, beaming with pride. 'Project Shakti is a huge success with over 60,000 women entrepreneurs. It is also taught as a case study at Harvard. Professor C. K. Prahalad spent a day with my team in Nalgonda, interacting with the Shakti ammas.' It was Project Shakti that earned Pradeep the title of 'Father of Rural India' in Prof. Prahalad's book, *The Fortune at the Bottom of the Pyramid*.

## Development Sector as Career Choice

Pradeep is of the opinion that knowledge in the fields of engineering, management and medicine can be great assets in improving the design and implementation of social programmes. According to him, summer internships can generate great interest in students early on.

'In the 1990s, I discussed this idea with academicians, bureaucrats and corporates. The dean of S. P. Jain College in Mumbai supported the idea and sent seven of his students to MART to work on a haat study. The students were thereby sensitized to the problems of rural India and a couple of them even expressed their desire to work in the rural sector.' Pradeep describes such a response as 'moving'.

He goes on to share a touching incident involving one of the student interns. 'One of the seven students from S. P. Jain working in Kalahandi – the most backward district of Orissa – came down with malaria and high fever. The closest primary centre was a kilometre away. The villagers put her on a *charpai* and carried her all the way there. She narrated the incident to me in tears, describing how complete strangers saved her life. It left an impression on her which she will never forget.'

The biggest roadblock for people joining the social work sector, according to Pradeep, is the salary difference as compared to the private sector. 'Fortunately, in recent years, we have seen a lot of hiring in rural divisions and CSR activities. Donor agencies and international NGO salaries are much better today.' The MART founder sees this as a trade-off between salary and personal satisfaction. Ending on a hopeful note, Pradeep shares, 'I see many more youngsters opting for social sector jobs today compared to the time I entered the sector in 1988.'

## Rural vs Urban Consumer

In Pradeep's view rural consumers today are at par with their urban counterparts in terms of aspirations and comfort with technology. 'The new rural consumer is the smartphone-savvy youth. The rural per capita income which used to be 50 percent of its urban counterpart, stands at 75 percent of the urban per capita income today.' Pradeep finds it interesting that the purchasing power of both the rural and the urban sectors are now comparable. This is because there is hardly any outflow on rent, water, electricity, education and medical expenses. Rural purchasing power matching its urban counterpart is the primary reason for the newfound interest in rural consumers.

## The Moral North Star

'Compassion, love and empathy,' Pradeep is quick to respond when asked about the moral values he swears by. 'You won't do any wrong if you feel for others. When we become compassionate, we realize we are all one,' says Pradeep with a confidence that comes from a life lived by these morals.

'When a child falls sick, it is the mother's love that heals the child, not the medicine. Medicine is just one part of it. We have to take compassion to a level where you empathize with your consumer. Look at the best inventors, and you will realize that they worked with relentless passion for the benefit of the community. This resulted in innovative discoveries. My advice to the young guns looking to win the rural markets is to empathize with the rural consumer, understand their needs and then design solutions with burning passion.'

## Back to BITS

'I didn't know a soul in BITS when I took admission. Belonging to an affluent family in Delhi and having grown up in a modern city, I was aghast to learn that there were no movie halls, no restaurants and no big shops in Pilani. There was only Gupta ji's shop selling samosas and dosas,' says Pradeep as he remembers taking some time to get used to these changes. 'When I arrived, I realized my room had not been swept in two days. I immediately went to the warden and complained "The sweeper hasn't come in two days!" He handed me a broom and said, "The sweeper has come."'

'Pilani was a great equalizer where the rich and the poor, south Indians and north Indians, government and private school students, all coexisted happily.' Pradeep credits BITS for his metamorphosis from a shy boy to a 'reasonably confident young man'. The college played a salient role in him becoming a resourceful individual.

'I cried on day one of entering BITS, cursing my luck. At the end of five years, when I left Pilani, I cried again – this time, because I would miss all my friends. We had created a special bond and friendship for life. I think, at that impressionable age, it left a deep, positive impression on my psyche.'

# AGE IS NO EXCUSE

## Prem Jain, Co-founder and CEO, Pensando Systems

Prem Jain is the CEO and co-founder of Pensando Systems, a cloud and enterprise data center startup launched in 2017 by four former executives of Cisco Systems. Prior to founding Pensando Systems, Jain spent twenty-three years as part of a team of engineers, who were financed by Cisco Systems to create innovative new startups. Known as the 'heart, soul and brains' of Cisco, the team was given wide latitude and formed several successful businesses bankrolled by the company. Later, these new ventures were bought back for significantly more money when they hit financial mileposts. The team and their startups were behind every breakout product created by Cisco in the past two decades.

Prem joined Cisco in 1993 as the director of Engineering when Cisco acquired Crescendo Communications, where he had been the vice president of Systems Architecture. At Crescendo, he was also responsible for the design and development of the firm's FDDI products as well as the first LAN switch, now known as the Cisco Catalyst 1200. Most recently, Prem served as the senior vice president and general manager of Cisco's Insieme Business Unit.

Prem is the recipient of two patents and is a member of the Institute of Electrical and Electronics Engineers (IEEE). He holds a BE degree with honours from BITS Pilani (1968–73) and a master's degree in Electrical and Computer Sciences from University of California, Davis (1975–77).

## Going the Corporate Way

AFTER GRADUATING FROM BITS PILANI IN 1973, PREM DECIDED to pursue a master's degree in computer science from UC Davis, to become a teacher. Upon completing his postgraduate studies, he received an offer from Bell-Northern Research, a Canada-based telecommunications company. Although he was reluctant at first, his advisor at the university urged him to work for a year to get some practical experience, suggesting that pursuing a PhD afterwards would be much more meaningful.

'I took his advice and joined Bell, but I never went back to pursue a PhD, even though I always wanted to do it. I still want to do it, if I get an opportunity, maybe I just might,' chuckles Prem.

After working for Bell for seven years, Prem started a company called David Systems, along with Mario Mazzalo and Luca Cafiero. 'Even though the venture was unsuccessful, it was a great learning experience for us. We had raised a significant amount of money from venture capital and had built a third-generation integrated Data and Voice PABX equipment product using voice, data and radio technologies. However, it wasn't a cost-effective solution for our clients. So despite being innovative, our product didn't click. Our biggest mistake was not assessing the market correctly, but it was a great learning curve for us and one which gave birth to our next company in 1989 – Crescendo Communications.' He adds, 'It is very important to focus on solving the current problems of the customer when you start out. You cannot be too early and you can't be too late either. With Crescendo, we were just in time because it was launched at the right time and tackled relevant consumer problems using modern technologies.'

## The Cisco Connection

When another opportunity came knocking in 1993, Prem and his co-founders were quick to grab hold of it. Cisco – an American network hardware company – was looking to acquire a company working with network switches and Crescendo had caught their eye. Their venture was successfully acquired by Cisco, the same year. 'We worked at Cisco and forged our business for the next decade and grew it to almost $15 billion, after which we decided to start up in 2001.' At Cisco, the Crescendo trio inducted Soni Jiandani into their team and launched Andiamo – which means 'let's go' in Italian – to tap into the SAN (Storage Area Network) switch market. This team of four later came to be known as the formidable 'MPLS' at Cisco. As Andiamo began to take its first steps, Cisco stepped in and took them and the startup under their wing. With that, Andiamo became a spin-in for Cisco.

In a spin-in arrangement refers, a company funds an internal startup, so that the people associated with it (who are the employees of that firm) can focus solely on building the product for the startup. 'Once the product is launched, the parent company buys it. Cisco allowed us to rent the space within the company itself. They funded the whole thing, and we seamlessly built the product,' explains Prem.

## MPLS

Though Mario, Prem and Luca had been working together since 1983, the MPLS quartet came into being when Soni joined them at Cisco. 'We have been working with each other for a very long time and the reason behind our success as a team is that we have great chemistry among us. Chemistry is the most important requirement for a successful team.' Prem believes that complementary skills and non-overlapping responsibilities help a team function more effectively. 'Soni handles marketing, which complements the three of us, who are hardcore tech guys.' In 2017, MPLS launched their latest startup, Pensando Systems, which delivers highly programmable software-defined cloud, computing, networking, storage and security services, with Prem as the CEO.

When asked about the commonalities between the members of MPLS, Prem adds, 'We are two Italians and two Indians, and there are a lot of things which we have in common. I think Italians, as well as Indians, have family-oriented cultures, and both love to eat good food. At Pensando, which we are currently building, all four of us eat our meals together. My wife cooks really well and Mario and Luca too are fond of the Indian dishes she prepares for our lunch.'

## String of Successes

'Our first spin-in together, Andiamo, was very successful. The company made a revenue of almost $500 million. We could have made several millions of dollars from this venture by selling it to Cisco but we chose not to and took up senior leadership roles in Cisco until 2005. Around 2005, Cisco wanted us to get the company into the server business and that's how we did another spin-in – Nuova Systems. We delivered a product called UCF which became very successful. The overall revenue coming out of that particular product, even today, is close to four billion dollars a year! I am glad to say that we became number one in the blade server market within three years after we launched the product, which was a huge feat.'

After the incredible success of Andiamo and Nuova, MPLS turned its attention to technology transitions, and decided to catch that particular wave again in 2011 with software-defined networking (SDN). Prem remembers how Cisco stepped in once again, 'When Cisco came to know that we were working on this technology, they wanted this to be another spin-in arrangement – we went ahead and started building Insieme Networks. In this case, we delivered a product called Application Centric Infrastructure (ACI) and delivered an SDN solution which was much better than any other SDN solution present in the market, as it offered complete visibility and integrated management of physical and virtual networked IT resources, and the product became very successful.'

The MPLS team left Cisco in 2016, and by that time, Insieme Networks – Cisco's attempt to redefine its SDN position – was generating close to $3 billion. 'With a lot of hard work, a great team, customer understanding, technical expertise and a little bit of luck, Insieme proved to be a fruitful endeavour,' says Prem about their last venture with Cisco.

## Spin-ins and Startups

Prem states that the concept of a spin-in is unique to the Bay area. 'It has a lot of advantages because the founders of the spin-in understand the company and what it expects from the product. One doesn't need to worry about building a sales, marketing or HR division, but only on building one's prototype while the parent company handles the rest.' He finds it to be an interesting way for a multinational company to enter new avenues or expand to adjacent areas of business.

He is quick to share the disadvantages as well. 'The major disadvantage, and also part of the reason why several big tech companies cannot do it, is that it can create a rift amongst the employees.' He had a similar experience at Cisco, where the leadership was often asked, 'Why are you letting MPLS do it and not other people?' He points out that it might make some employees jealous because of the monetary benefits that accompany the success of the spin-ins. 'There are both negatives and positive sides. For us, the positive side of this whole story was that we created almost 70–80 billion-dollar businesses for the company.' Prem claims that the spin-in model is uncommon even in the US, owing to the risky nature of the venture. 'In India, the amount of funding a typical startup receives is much less compared to their American counterparts. In the last five years, the Indian startup ecosystem has changed tremendously,' says Prem, urging young entrepreneurs to trust their gut and take the plunge.

## Love for Travelling

Prem has been an avid traveller since his college days. As a first-year student at BITS, he concocted a 'crazy' plan along with a close friend to hitchhike to Europe. 'After flying to Kabul from Amritsar, we changed a few buses to reach Iran, from where we hitchhiked all the way to London. We went on to do this every summer of college. Each time, we included more friends from our batch, and at one time, there were eight of us, so we divided ourselves into groups and decided on rendezvous points. On one of these trips, we all got part-time jobs in Darmstadt with the help of Prof. Wendel, who taught German at BITS at the time. We worked for two weeks and managed to earn enough money to sponsor our trip.'

Prem is also a deft mountain climber. He has scaled the summits of mountains such as Mt Whitney, which is at 14,500 ft above sea level, and explored iconic sites like Machu Picchu and the Grand Canyon. Age is just a number for Prem, who is now in his seventies and dreams of climbing Mt Kailash in India and Mt Kilimanjaro in Africa. 'I go for a hike almost every day, if I can. There is a hill behind my house called Mission Peak. I try to go there every day at 5:00 a.m. and come back by 6:30 a.m. on weekdays and take another half hour on weekends.'

## Age Is No Excuse

Prem believes that an individual is capable of learning from any person and any situation, given one has the will to do so. 'Keep yourself active, don't use your age as an excuse,' says Prem on the back of a career that has spanned over five decades. He urges the younger generation to be unfazed by failure, and even by success. 'Focus on making an impact, do it for your community, your family, for the world. Becoming rich is secondary, and it will happen. But one should aim to make their life happier.' A proponent of giving back to the community, he insists that it's never too late or never too less to give back. Furthermore, he asserts the importance of taking time out for oneself. 'If you need to unwind, don't wait, thinking you'll do it when you're old. If you want to travel, travel now, because when you are older, you might not be able to do a lot of things which you dreamt of.' Prem considers people around him to be his greatest wealth and prioritizes relationships with the people he cares about over everything else.

## Back to BITS

Prem describes his college friendships and memories as everlasting ones. 'You might lose touch with your college friends but even when you meet them after decades, you'd feel like you never left Pilani.'

A tireless supporter of BITS and a great mentor for countless BITSians, he has been deeply involved with the college's alumni association BITSAA, since its early days and has led countless initiatives for the community. 'Today, the organization works for a plethora of issues. Through alumni funds, it aims to give back to the alma mater by providing state-of-the-art infrastructure and the latest technology. There are four beneficiaries – students, faculty, locals in Pilani and retired college staff.' Prem played an instrumental role in launching the BITSConnect initiative. 'As part of the initiative, we used fibre optics to wire every faculty home, so they could use voiceover IP phones, instead of using regular phones. With this wireless network, we have established connections across Shivganga to the museum to the library, to all the bhawans. We were able to ensure connectivity to the outside world in every room. The idea was to bring higher bandwidth to BITS Pilani. And then we also launched BITSConnect 2.0, through which we brought video conferencing technologies to each BITS campus to build India's first virtual classrooms. They are called telepresence rooms. It became very successful, and it is very much in demand at BITS.'

His contributions to the institution are an expression of his heartfelt desire to support his alma mater. 'I wish everyone at BITS Pilani a successful career, and if there is any way that the BITSians here in Silicon Valley can be of help, they only have to let us know. I hope BITS alumni continuously go and give back to BITS as much as possible. We must inculcate this thought amongst all students, so that as alumni, they too look back and think about what they can do for BITS.'

# KEEP MARCHING ON

## Sagar Yarnalkar, Co-founder and CEO, DailyNinja

Raised in a business family from Thane, Maharashtra, Sagar graduated from BITS Goa in 2012 with a dual degree in BE Electrical and Electronics and MSc Economics. Sagar worked at Reflexis and Carwale.com in tech roles before starting his first company in 2014, called Scoot – an app that integrated cab aggregators like Ola, Uber, TaxiforSure and Meru, among others. After his stint at Scoot, Sagar and his college friend, Anurag Gupta, started DailyNinja – India's largest early morning milk and grocery delivery service – in 2015. The firm was backed by Sequoia Capital, Matrix Partners India, Saama Capital, Whiteboard Capital and angel investors, including the likes of Kunal Shah, Aprameya Radhakrishna and Anupam Mittal. In 2020, DailyNinja was acquired by BigBasket and the company still remains one of India's biggest grocery delivery companies, for which Sagar was featured by *Forbes Asia* and *India* in their '30 Under 30' 2019 list. Currently with BigBasket as an 'entrepreneur in residence', Sagar is also an active angel investor looking to back promising early-stage companies in India.

## Building DailyNinja

IN JANUARY 2014, SAGAR LEFT HIS JOB AT CARWALE.COM AND started Scoot – an aggregator app for cab aggregators like Ola, Uber, TaxiforSure, Meru and others in the market at that time. Scoot was popular when India had many cab companies but with the consolidation in this space, only Ola and Uber were left standing. Aggregating for just two major cab players didn't seem viable. So he exited from Scoot and sold the product to a Bangalore-based software product company. Unfazed by this initial setback and constantly motivated by his business-oriented family, Sagar decided to take another plunge into the world of entrepreneurship with Anurag Gupta (also from BITS Goa), when he saw the hyper-local delivery sector heat up. They invested the money earned from Scoot and from making software products for other startups in a new venture to acquire initial scale. Thus was born DailyNinja.

By 2020, DailyNinja was flourishing with a workforce of 2,000 milkmen. This was not the case when Sagar Yarnalkar, along with Anurag, first developed their milk delivery app. 'Anurag and I would personally deliver milk to our customers. That's how we kept the firm afloat for the first three months. Even today, when we have an impressive network of milkmen, Anurag and I often go for deliveries once a week to observe how our operations are being carried out.' Sagar feels it's important for them to be aware of what's happening at the grassroots as founders. This aids them in identifying any issues and fixing them as needed. 'The biggest inefficiencies in an organization arise when there is a communication gap. Once we fix it, the organization works as one unit.'

Transparent communication goes a long way, as Sagar would attest. He accredits bagging early investors to the firm's honest pitch. 'We didn't try to bluff. We gave the investors a clear picture and just fine-tuned our goals with passing time, and our investors appreciated the honesty.' This honesty and vigour helped Anurag and Sagar build a formidable business, which was acquired by BigBasket in 2020.

## Metrics and Ownership

Sagar consistently attempts to instil a feeling of ownership in his team, urging them to rely on solid metrics to measure their progress. Along with keeping track of their work, the employees must also be aligned with the vision of the company and the founder.

'In a startup, time is money,' quips Sagar. 'An employee is paid according to the time they dedicate to the company. So the vision is that everyone thinks in the way that I do or how the senior management does. Everyone should have clarity on what is expected of them. That is the biggest challenge we face and this is what I am trying to work on.' Sagar rightly states that with the relevant metrics in place, it is easier to make sense of the efforts and output.

## Overcoming Adversity

Over the years, DailyNinja has overcome many challenges to earn the success it enjoys today. In March 2017, the company had run out of funds and was on the verge of shutting down. Sagar remembers it as the toughest time of his tenure. He was living hand to mouth and even had to sell his car.

'I took a loan of ₹40 lakh and tried to make sure the firm survives for the next four to five months.' Eventually, they managed to pull through and Sagar learned a valuable lesson from the experience. 'I might be considered naïve, and rightly so, because if I was told to do that again, I would not. There is a fine line between passion and madness, and I realize now that I shouldn't have taken such a major monetary risk. I was lucky that things worked out for me.'

## The Business Model

Sagar explains that DailyNinja works on monopolizing the items used most frequently by an average Indian household.

'In India, it's milk – an item that is purchased every day. We were able to expand our business after successfully engaging and retaining the milk-purchasing customers.' He describes this business model as an attempt to partner with the milkmen and onboard their existing customers to an online platform. They did this with milkmen in Bangalore and assembled their own warehouse management team.

'When money was tight,' recollects Sagar, 'I tried to find someone else who could handle the warehousing for us. Someone who required a warehouse and could generate value from it. This model would work for us, as well as him. With this, the costs came down drastically and someone else was earning from it too. These two things played out really well for us. They were major learning points and helped us mature our model.'

By April 2019, DailyNinja had bumped up their orders from 5,000 a day to over 80,000 orders daily. 'Now we feel that our next milestone should target 10 lakh orders a day,' says a hopeful Sagar.

## The DailyNinjas

Explaining why milkmen choose to partner with his company, Sagar says, 'Apart from the monetary incentive, the milkmen have the benefit of foregoing the monthly headache of door-to-door cash collection as 90 percent of the bills are paid online. Earlier, they would come to know about the amount of milk their buyers required only when they visited the house, which meant there was always an excess or shortfall. DailyNinja solves this problem by predetermining the required quantity of milk to help save the milkmen time and money and thereby increases their efficiency multifold.'

## Starting Up

'All three of us – MilkBasket, Doodhwaala and DailyNinja started around the same time. The competition further heated up when the big guys such as Swiggy and BigBasket started showing interest. The latter reached out to us in 2018.' The rising competition worked in DailyNinja's favour, points out Sagar. 'Investors needed validation to put money, and the interest these big companies displayed validated this space.' DailyNinja has grown substantially since then, making two key acquisitions the same year – Wakeup Basket and 4AM. 'Acquisitions are always tricky – both the culture and the vision of the parties involved must be aligned. For us, both acquisitions worked out well. 4AM was a pure transfer of assets. Straightforward and simple. On the other hand, Wakeup Basket was an acquisition of both team and assets, with their founder also joining us. His views aligned with ours and it seemed like an organic fit. We had luck on our side and the founder was a great addition to our team,' explains Sagar.

## Success Mantra

Sagar trusts in an array of values that guided him career-wise. 'You have to be able to adjust, and you need to have an open mind.' He feels a venture based on persistence and diligence is bound to be a meaningful undertaking. 'You need IQ and EQ. You don't know what will happen tomorrow. So when required, keep your emotions aside and move forward with your objectives. Just don't cry over spilt milk and keep marching on.'

He also mentions how working on his fitness has helped him build his persistence. His father had got him a gym membership after he completed his twelfth grade. 'The initial two months were tough but later, it became a habit. I was very competitive and tried to lift more weight than the other people of my age in the gym and this habit stuck with me at BITS. I was the only guy who used to go every day, even during the exams. This has helped develop a sense of discipline in me.'

## Significant Other in Business

While many startups have shut down because of conflict and ego clashes among the founders, Sagar and Anurag have run DailyNinja together for nearly six years now. 'Anurag and I, we have our arguments too, but we know that we have to work together, and hence, we have to stick it out. I have known him for the past twelve years. We accept each other's views and try to find the middle ground.' A trustworthy co-founder by his side allows Sagar to take a break when he needs to. 'When you have a co-founder, you can switch off for some time. Anurag knows that I switch off my phone and sleep at 11:00 p.m. and there is no issue. I return the missed calls as soon as I wake up.

Cooperating with each other allows both of us to take some time off and this helps us significantly.'

He is grateful for the understanding between them, which means that neither of them feels overworked. 'We are open with each other, and we make sure we communicate well, and often. I know exactly what work he has allotted to everyone. And when he's on leave, I know what work has to be done,' shares a content Sagar with a piece of important advice for co-founders everywhere: 'Be cognizant of your partner's work and be empathetic towards one another.'

## Back to BITS

When Sagar entered college as a first-year student, the Goa campus was only three years old. It did have the same festivals (cultural, technical and sports), clubs and departments as the one in Rajasthan. 'Funnily enough, I was shortlisted for the same branch at both the campuses. At that age, I only wanted to have fun and hence chose to go to Goa.' shares Sagar candidly. 'So I didn't do much academically once I realized attending classes wasn't compulsory.'

It was in his second year of college that Sagar had his first fling with entrepreneurship, when he and Anurag advertised that they were selling colours around campus for Holi and sold coupons for the mess grub. 'The coupons for the mess grub were free and you would be allotted one of the two messes, CH-4 and AH-4. CH-4 was the girls' mess and the more preferred one. Now, the slot to avail coupons for CH-4 would be opened only on one particular day. So Anurag and I, along with a couple of our friends, would book coupons for that particular slot, ahead of others and then sell it to other boys who wanted to go to the girls' mess on the day of the grub for ₹500.' They didn't mind going to the other mess because the premium fetched by those coupons felt lucrative to them. In some ways, these small initiatives and fun schemes improved their business acumen.

Sagar did not participate in any club or department activities initially and spent most of his time hanging out with his friends, going to the gym or playing one sport or the other. But in his second year, he ended up joining the Department of Publicity and Public Relations (DePP). Though the work allotted to him that year didn't interest him much, he worked diligently. His hard work paid off and he became a co-head of the department, the following year – a gig that gave him an early opportunity to hone his management skills – and the rest, as they say, is history.

# THINK, DO, BE

## Sandhya Prakash, Founder and MD, Beacon Energy Solutions

Sandhya Prakash is an entrepreneur, environmentalist, singer and spiritual artist. With over twenty-five years of business development and entrepreneurial experience across India and the Middle East, Sandhya has balanced work alongside pursuing her hobbies. She is the founder and managing director of Beacon, an energy management and renewable energy company, which has helped over eighty organizations to reduce their electricity consumption by over 40 percent per client in the UAE.

During her time at BITS Pilani (1987–91), Sandhya pursued a master's degree in Management Studies. As the first woman chairperson of the global BITS Alumni Association (BITSAA), she led the 54,000-strong organization between 2017–20. She is a motivational speaker and has addressed various forums around the world, like TEDx, Vegetarian Advocacy and Sustainability Panels.

Alongside her personal practices of yoga and meditation, Sandhya is a certified Tamara Energy (Japanese alignment technique) practitioner and has been a Ho'Oponopono (Hawaiian practice of reconciliation and forgiveness) practitioner for over ten years and has impacted over 400 individuals to be better versions of themselves.

## Narora Days

SANDHYA COMES FROM NARORA – THE PLACE WHERE THE FIRST atomic power plant in Uttar Pradesh was established in 1977. 'My father was an electrical engineer who was heading the electrical division at the plant. Narora is in western UP – an area plagued by dacoits back then. Needless to mention, we had to be wary of these threats. Fortunately, I never experienced that side of Narora and only remember it as the city through which the Ganges passes. It brought me close to nature.' This love for nature and concern for the environment has stayed with her to date.

She remembers being fiercely competitive as a young student in school. 'I always had to be there at the top, coming second was never an option for me. The influence of my grandmother in this respect is strong. In fact, when I meet my school friends now, they tell me how they hated me for coming first every time then, but now they tell their kids to study like I did and use me as an example.' Slightly embarrassed at her competitiveness as a grown-up, Sandhya discloses that her parents never pressured her into studying, and the competitive spirit she had was innate. Instead, her parents encouraged her to be expressive of her desires and always urged her to work towards them.

## India to Saudi

Sandhya graduated from BITS at the cusp of Indian liberalization with multinationals pouring in with lucrative job offers. 'There were more jobs than students,' says Sandhya. 'There weren't many reputable institutions back then, and BITSians were the first choice for all firms. I was offered a job at Wipro and another at Mastek.' Although Wipro offered a significantly higher salary than the amount offered by Mastek, Sandhya chose to work with the latter. 'It was a smaller company that offered relatively more practical experience. There was more room for growth and learning.' Even with firms flooding the BITS campus with job offers, a majority of the students from the graduating batch went for their master's abroad. Sandhya worked for Mastek in Delhi for a year and shifted base to Hyderabad later. After getting married, she moved to Saudi Arabia to be with her husband, who worked there. 'Middle East was a completely different experience. Our plan was to stay in Saudi for two years, but then it turned out to be eleven years in Saudi and now fifteen in Dubai.'

Though Saudi Arabia has opened up to the idea of women entering the workspace today, it wasn't the case when Sandhya moved to the country in 1993. She wasn't allowed to work at most firms, which made her doubt her decision to shift to Saudi. 'It was an issue back then, but I managed to pull through by having a positive approach, being flexible, and also with the support of my husband. I didn't allow that thought to linger in my mind for too long. I did a couple of correspondence courses from Birmingham University and then from University of Pennsylvania, USA.' She also did a few courses on merchandising, marketing, clothing and textiles, and started her own company in India before deciding to become her own boss. 'I got myself a partner based out of Saudi and that's how I strategized to get into different businesses in Saudi Arabia. First as an agency and then as a full-fledged company.'

'This period was also personally transformational as I balanced motherhood and business. The experience of motherhood was deeply spiritual and enabled me to get in touch with myself and my vulnerabilities. Celebration of the nuances of emotions and centering oneself showed me how to continuously think, do and be.'

After witnessing the gender divide in Saudi Arabia in the 1990s and seeing the transformation the country is going through today, Sandhya has learnt that with time, everything changes. 'I have realized that persistence and consistency always pay off in the long run.'

## Plans for BITSAA

Joining the BITS Alumni Association (BITSAA) was a turning point in Sandhya's life. The memorable years she spent in Pilani have chiselled her personality. Her brush with BITSAA came in 2001, after the World Trade Centre towers came down. Sandhya and her son had visited the place just a week before the terror attack. She recalls how back in Saudi, as she was getting out of jetlag, they had watched the towers crumble on TV. 'Three of my batchmates started BITSAA in the US after this incident, to help fellow BITSians. In parallel, I decided to support them and bring together a network of BITSians in the Middle East. Dubai already had an active chapter, and we formed a Yahoo! Group in 2002.'

The power of networking, the impact her alma mater had on her and the encouragement of the former chairpersons, motivated Sandhya to step up as the global chairperson in 2017. She envisions an integrated approach for BITSAA based on a strong foundation with the US and India arms working in tandem to formalize the organization. She sees this as the most effective way to give back to her alma mater. According to Sandhya, a community is as strong as its members. 'One should conceptualize a vision, and everyone must be able to agree with it. Great things happen when members of a community take ownership of it. India has several BITSAA chapters and as a member of its executive team, I have been involved in helping streamline its functioning. BITSAA's success is primarily because of the innate sense of camaraderie among the alumni and our shared love for BITS. We want to define roles and responsibilities in a way that BITSAA continues to operate seamlessly, irrespective of the people in charge of running it.' She believes that every chapter is equally important and hopes to turn it into a truly global association.

While the organization's goal is to raise funds for the institution and improve its facilities, Sandhya doesn't want BITSAA to interfere with the college's functioning. 'BITS is doing an excellent job as an educational institution. We want to support the alumni and students, in terms of jobs, counselling, career growth and industry experience. Our goal is to provide students with industry experience early on.'

## Energy Conservation

An environmentalist to the core, Sandhya notes with concern that in 2019, Earth Overshoot Day fell on 29 July. In 2020, it was on 22 August. Earth Overshoot Day marks the date when humanity has exhausted nature's budget for the year. She elaborates, 'For the rest of the year, we create an ecological deficit by drawing from local resource stocks and accumulating carbon dioxide in the atmosphere. Until a couple of decades ago, the date used to fall in November. Our population is growing at an exceptional pace, and we are consuming resources as rapidly. We need nine times the total resources available on earth to sustain consumption at this pace. By draining these resources, we're borrowing from the next few years.'

In India, explains Sandhya, the sheer size of the population calls for an urgent need to shift to using renewable resources. 'Most of India's coal is imported from Australia, and only meagre percentages of energy can be extracted from coal, especially after significant reduction via transmission losses and transportation.' This means to meet the country's energy requirements we end up depleting non-renewable resources at a dangerously fast rate. Elaborating on the need to be pre-emptive about conserving our resources, Sandhya says, 'Nobody cared till there was a water crisis in Chennai, and suddenly there was chaos all around. Similar catastrophe is ready to strike all major Indian cities, unless we pledge to shift to renewable energy sources *now*.' She has been focussing her efforts on plantation drives, discussing a greener future on numerous forums and evangelizing people who have the power to work for this noble cause.

## Beacon of Hope

Sandhya firmly believes that the power to save the planet lies with the people. 'We have to do our best to protect the five elements – wind, water, fire, earth, and space. The air is polluted, so is water, the planet is getting hotter by the day, the topsoil is getting eroded faster than ever, and space debris is another issue altogether with tonnes of garbage being dumped into the outer space.' Yet, Sandhya is optimistic about the future and places her trust in the younger generation, stating that they care much more about the environment than their parents' generation. 'They are extremely innovative and that's why I prefer working with youngsters.'

Sandhya's love for nature led her to found Beacon Energy Solutions. Elaborating on her vision for the company, she says, 'I want to help people live a more sustainable and eco-friendly life. We took on one simple goal – to reduce water and electric bills in the Middle East. The company has undertaken a lot of projects at the grassroots level in the five years of its existence. We have developed a process called Monitoring Audit Retrofit and Solar (MARS) for the fast adoption of energy-saving retrofits and renewable energy solutions across industries and commercial and residential buildings. One should try to think of saving the environment as a holistic effort that involves looking at both the biological and chemical dimensions of nature. We have new technologies coming up – some that have the potential to extract potable water from water vapour in the air. There has been a lot of work done to tap into solar energy too.'

Sandhya is a strong proponent of a sustainable circular economy and recommends an urgent change in attitude towards the environment. 'Sustainability is a long-term goal, but our thinking makes it seem like a short-term goal. The long-term thinking process is very different, and we really need to change our attitude, especially in India. We need to encourage people to take collective responsibility for the planet we live on and pace the use of resources based on need rather than greed.'

'In the 1800s, the society dealt with slavery, in the 1900s we worked for the upliftment of women and this century would be devoted to animal care and environmental conservation. That's why I began popularizing plant-based food in the Middle East.' Sandhya formed the Middle East Vegetarian Group (MEVEG) as a volunteer group in 2007. 'Keeping religious sentiments aside, simply from the viewpoint of sustainability and animal welfare, plant-based foods are a necessity today. Over 56 billion animals are killed every year, just for human consumption and that is why we need to adopt a vegetarian lifestyle.' Sandhya is immensely proud to be a part of the International Vegetarian Union UK – as a representative in the Middle East to promote a vegan way of living.

## Word to the Wise

Sandhya believes in finding a balance between the creative and the analytical through art. 'The right hemisphere of the human brain works on technical and analytical processing, and to balance it, the left brain should be engaged in creative activities. This is where art comes in. I have started painting with my fingers. It's called energy art. I wanted to feel the paint. It's really peaceful and relaxing, and I have made about ninety paintings.'

In her experience as an entrepreneur, Sandhya has identified that communication is key to building a successful venture. 'Founders should discuss their thought process clearly with each and every stakeholder – be it their own team, an investor or the users.' She advises entrepreneurs to meticulously chart out an elaborate three-year plan which would help them understand how economically viable their ideas are. 'One should also know when to exit. There might be a venture that achieves a similar end goal, don't try to play and catch up with them. Drop it and start something else. I can give you other tips, but at the end of the day, you should listen to your gut. Go with your instincts.'

Sandhya, without hesitating, mentions the importance of strong core values such as integrity, which she believes is an 'all-encompassing' trait. 'Aim to have integrity, and you will have a meaningful life.'

## Back to BITS

Sandhya joined BITS in 1987 and affirms that the four years that followed were the best years of her life. BITS was quite different from Narora, where she had spent most of her life, but she gradually found her tribe in college. 'I learnt a lot from my roommates. These were people from Chennai, Delhi and other metropolitan cities. So for the first two semesters, I would just be sitting and listening to their stories.' Although their lifestyle came as a cultural shock to her, she found the experience of listening to them to be transformative.

'When I entered BITS, I didn't join any clubs for a year. Then in my third semester, I auditioned and got into the

Music Club. I sang two songs at my first "Music Nite". It went very well and I still remember it vividly.' The Music Club and the friends she made there hold a special place in her heart. They remain in touch even today.

She was actively involved in the management festival called 'Interface' and kick-started a competition called the Pilani Stock Exchange. 'I didn't know a lot about stocks at that time, but I learned along the way.' She also developed an interest in birdwatching and ornithology while in college and says that it is one of the few hobbies she still actively pursues. 'We started a club called the Cuckoo Club. Over a span of two years, we identified over 250 birds. All these migratory birds would be on their way to Bharatpur and we would be present at the Birla Gliding Club at five in the morning to spot them. And on top of that, the members of the club were given special permission to leave the campus at 4 a.m. to go to Bharatpur Sanctuary. Usually, no girls would be allowed to get out of the hostel at that hour.' The Cuckoo Club organized the first-ever exhibition at APOGEE and motivated many volunteers from junior batches to pursue this hobby.

At the silver jubilee reunion of her batch in 2015, she got the chance to relive her college days. 'I visited our hostel, Meera Bhavan, sang at the music night curated for our batchmates, walked to the erstwhile gliding club and watched birds and the sunrise, stayed at the guesthouse in a dorm, ate mess food and visited C'not for old times' sake.' She admits to having a lot of gratitude for BITS Pilani as it bestowed upon her the blessings of friends, the character of resilience and a thirst for lifelong learning.

# STAND FOR WHAT YOU BELIEVE IN

## Shishir Joshipura, MD and CEO, Praj Industries Ltd

Equipped with a bachelor's degree in Mechanical Engineering from BITS Pilani and an Advanced Management Programme (AMP) from Harvard Business School, Shishir started his professional journey as a trainee engineer with Thermax in 1983. After spending twenty-six years at Thermax, he became the CEO of SKF India. In April 2018, Shishir took over as the CEO and MD of Praj Industries Ltd, a Pune-based industrial biotech major.

He served on the board of Process Plant and Machinery Association of India (PPMAI) as the director and chairman from 2007 to 2009 and is the founding director of Alliance for Energy-Efficient Economy (AEEE) – an industry think tank and policy advocacy organization for energy efficiency in India. He has served as the chairperson of CII Pune Zone (2015–16) and has been a speaker at Harvard Business School India Forum on two occasions. Shishir has also served two terms as the independent Director on the board of SBI Mutual Funds (2012–17). He is currently the co-chairman of the CII National Task Force on Bioenergy (2020–21) and also a member of the governing board of the Council of EU Chambers of Commerce in India.

In 2013, Shishir was named one of the most valuable CEOs of India by *Business World* and listed amongst 'India's Top 100 CEOs in 2013' by *Business Today*.

## Childhood in the Pink City

SHISHIR HAS HAD A UNIQUE UPBRINGING FOR HIS GENERATION – being an only child with both his parents working was uncommon in the 1960s. 'Having two working parents wasn't the norm, back then. When I returned from school, there would be no one at home. I learnt to be independent and yet be interdependent from a very early age. I had a very happy childhood and those really were simpler times.' Shishir deeply appreciates the love and affection his parents showered on him. He also has immense respect for the meaningful struggles they undertook, without ever giving up on their ambitions. 'My constantly remind me that I, and only I, was accountable for my actions.'

'We were a Gujarati family living in Rajasthan, and I had friends who hailed from different parts of the country. It never crossed our minds whether somebody was Christian or Muslim, or from south India or north India. What mattered was that we were having fun. I vividly remember one of my south Indian friends who had just returned from the USA. He did not know Hindi and I did not know English – yet we used to hang out together outside of our respective school timings. He offered to share with me a couple of Hardy Boys books to help me improve my English. Several half-read books later, I became more comfortable with the language and also learned to communicate with him.'

'When I joined BITS Pilani, I realized it was one thing to read Hardy Boys and a completely different thing to read Resnick Halliday and G. B. Thomas. Initially, I struggled because my mind was thinking in Hindi and I was expected to write answers in English.'

## The Right Work Culture

According to Shishir, the work culture speaks volumes about an organization. 'Unlike other metrics, such as salaries or job descriptions, you come to know about the work culture only when you are a part of the organization,' says Shishir, who wholeheartedly believes that a work culture that reflects a sound value system is the very foundation of a great organization.

'Only a nurturing and supportive work culture can mould an open, transparent, honest and value-abiding leader. Culture plays the most important role in the professional life of a young graduate transitioning into the team-oriented corporate world from the individual-centric academic world. The culture you encounter and adopt at the beginning of your career also determines, to an extent, the kind of leader you would become later on.'

## Culture at Praj

'Praj is a unique organization – passionate and committed. With its value system serving as the bedrock, the organization has built a resilient "never say die" culture,' shares a proud Shishir, who has been a part of the company since 2018.

'At Praj, we consider investment into our human resources to be a critical pillar of our success. Training is an essential ingredient of the company's strong and continued investment in building technological prowess. We are aware that updating, renewing and applying knowledge holds the key to sustainable growth.'

On the evolving expectations from business leaders, Shishir comments, 'Today's leaders are expected to address and tackle challenges posed in an increasingly VUCA (volatile, uncertain, complex and ambiguous) world. They have to be agile, open, transparent and committed to their cause. And I want my leadership team to bring these qualities to the table. But most importantly, they should be the right cultural fit.'

## The Startup Connection

Praj was founded as a startup, and Shishir has continued to be a part of the startup ecosystem by starting numerous businesses in different domains. 'Over the years, I have had to do a great deal of conceiving, starting, running, falling, staying true to the vision and getting up again with these businesses. The experience helped me become more agile and customer-, people- and process-centric, while helping me become more appreciative of risks and their mitigation. I am sure many startup founders today have similar stories and experiences.'

## Saving the Future

For the longest time, Shishir has believed that renewable energy possesses the potential to build a sustainable future. 'Converting natural resources into commercially viable and usable forms of energy is a key battle for mankind. We have incorporated several unsustainable ways into our lifestyle, and it is most glaringly visible in our choice of primary energy resources in all walks of life. Fossil fuels are extracting a large and non-retractable cost from us. If we do not switch to sustainable options, we will end up compromising the future of our children.'

Shishir explains a possible way out of the impending crisis using the example of mobility – one of the most basic amenities. 'Any solution to address the future direction of mobility must be capable of addressing carbon footprint reduction, improved energy security, reduced foreign exchange outflow, reduced local air pollution and protection and growth of employment in both rural and industrial economies. Several alternatives are now available to address the challenge posed by fossil fuel combustion systems and there are many advanced economies in the world that are focusing on electrification of the fleet (e-mobility).'

## Bio-Mobility

Though Shishir quotes electrification as a likely solution to the problems created by fossil fuel combustion, he also points out a significant downside of e-mobility. 'An electric vehicle has only 700 parts, compared to 17,000 parts in an internal combustion engine (ICE) driven, equivalent vehicle. One cannot even imagine the impact of the evaporating employment opportunities and outcomes for the nation's economy. E-mobility will also call for significant investment in charging infrastructure, changes in the country's electrical energy generation infrastructure, continued dependence on imported raw material and pose a new environmental problem in the form of used battery disposal.'

To counter this, Praj has developed Bio-Mobility, a platform that envisages the use of renewable resources to produce carbon-neutral transportation fuel across all modes of mobility. The platform makes use of agri-residues and organic waste-derived biofuels in the form of ethanol, biodiesel, renewable biogas, sustainable aviation and marine fuel as primary energy sources for driving mobility while retaining basic ICE technology.

## Alliance for Energy-Efficient Economy (AEEE)

In 2000, Shishir stepped in as the CEO of Thermax Energy Performance Services (TEPS), an industrial energy services company. It was around this time that he met Hema Hattangady – then CEO of Conzerv – a recognized market leader in the electrical energy efficiency space in the Indian market. She liked what TEPS was attempting to do in the thermal energy space with regard to energy efficiency and wanted to explore if the same could be applied to the domain of electrical energy. Out of this common interest in doing something for the country in the field of energy efficiency, the AEEE was born in 2008. Shishir explains, 'There was no commercial angle to it. It was an industry think tank focused on the cause. Sustainable energy has always intrigued me.'

## The Art of Management

With a career spanning over three decades, Shishir has come to realize that the role of a leader is independent of the industry domain. 'I can't tell engineers at Praj how to build a world-class ethanol plant, neither suggest to the engineers at SKF how to make better bearings. The leader needs to be able to build on the good of the organization, tap into people's potential, help them dream and then empower them to realize it. It is essential as a leader to understand how customer value proposition can be enhanced by deploying the unique skill set of your team and aligning their efforts.'

Shishir observes that leadership issues across industries are similar in nature and it takes vision and collective effort to create a unique value proposition. 'It is fine for a leader to admit that they don't know something in particular, because it is impossible for one person to know everything. In a team, it is not about whether *I* know it or not, it is about whether *we* know it or not,' counsels Shishir.

## Harvard Advanced Management Program

In 2007, Shishir joined the Advanced Management Program (AMP) at Harvard Business School. AMP is a programme for senior executives with 20–25 years of experience from organizations with annual sales revenues of $250 million or more, which is built to hone the skills of top-hat business leaders and bless them with even wider professional perspectives.

He describes his experience at Harvard as 'unique', as the programme was designed to club participants with a diverse set of immensely competent individuals to ensure optimum learning. 'My group included the head of the Singapore army, MD of Goldman Sachs Australia, head of HR at Eastman, an entrepreneur from the Netherlands, a French banker posted in Korea and the president of Canada's largest bank. We came from different backgrounds and hence looked at things from varying perspectives. The goal of every assignment in the course was to develop a consolidated and holistic view when presented with a problem.' Shishir says he, along with his group, learned how to be open and respectful to contrary opinions. He used to work for about eighteen hours a day during the course of his studies at Harvard. 'The programme helped me appreciate different cultural perspectives. I would strongly recommend it to all senior executives. The purpose of the professors there is not to teach you, but to make you think.'

## Battling Recessions

'There's no such thing as a steady state in business anymore. Those days are gone; we are living in a much more complex world,' comments Shishir on the ups and downs of the business world. 'You cannot possibly factor in everything. One has to be cognizant of the fact that business cycles keep changing. It pays dividends to be proactive, and it's all about being market-driving and not market-driven.'

He feels that it is the leadership's responsibility to make sure that the organization is constantly evolving, with a view to create a long-term sustainable growth path and overcome short-term challenges. 'There might be times when the company doesn't perform as well as you want it to. Stay true to your vision and act with agility and empathy to overcome any adverse situation, and you'll sail through.'

It is also important to prioritize the long-term future of your organization. Sharing an example, Shishir recounts, 'When SKF was going through a difficult market situation, we practically cut every cost except the training budget. We felt that our people would fare better if they were trained to face emerging challenges, and they did!'

## Embrace Change for Success

Shishir attributes his professional success to being customer-centric. 'If a customer has an issue, I cannot rest,' confesses Shishir. 'If we have committed to a customer, we *must* deliver. Come what may. Customers expect us to be reliable as market leaders, and we must align all our capabilities and innovation to solve their problems.' Shishir takes great pride in his value system and never backs down from holding his ground in the face of crisis. 'It helps you in adverse times. Trust your value system sincerely. You have to be value-driven and stand for what you believe in and speak up.'

At Thermax, he was encouraged to speak up even as a trainee engineer. This is something Shishir practices and motivates others to do even today, that is build honest and healthy dialogue among colleagues. 'I tell my team that I will question you to understand the problem better, but I will never doubt you. I trust their judgement and urge them to express themselves freely. This brings positive energy to the company. There is no right view or wrong view. It is my view and your view; both may be valid from different perspectives. Keep on learning, ask more questions, learn more and experiment more,' says Shishir, who believes being passionately curious while respecting different views can be a game changer. 'Do not fear change, rather welcome it.'

Unwinding oneself to avoid burning out is a part of his success mantra. He has always been an avid reader and is particularly fond of reading autobiographies, books on management, technology and fiction. 'Apart from reading, I love spending time with my daughter and family. I also enjoy meeting my friends. Moreover, I don't do anything that I am not convinced about. That takes away half of my potential stress. I simply have less to worry about.'

## Back to BITS

In Shishir's opinion, BITS pushes its students to be decisive early on. 'Right or wrong, you are responsible for your decisions at BITS. You can find alternative paths, but you have to stay true to your goal. These are the things that actually count in the professional world: the ability to deal with ambiguity, the ability to make decisions and the ability to find alternatives while sticking to your goals. It builds a sense of accountability and flexibility in you and an ability to deal with things on a multi-cultural level. BITS is a place where many languages are spoken. These are some of the very great things that the institution teaches you.'

Shishir and his college friends make it a point to meet once a year. 'Our wives also get along well with each other. A few years ago, we went to Mahabaleshwar and the next year, to

Pilani. Now that our kids are getting married, so in any case we meet at their weddings.' One of his friends had joined the army and used to be posted to different cities across the country, which meant Shishir couldn't meet him for almost seventeen years. But their friendship remains as strong as ever. 'When his daughter got admission in a college in Pune, where I currently reside, my friend, who was posted in Jaipur at the time, remembered how much I love *ghewar* – a Rajasthani sweet – and made sure to send a box of the sweet with her,' fondly recollects Shishir. Among other things, he is grateful to his alma mater for friendships like this that have withstood the test of time.

# DO WHAT CHALLENGES YOU

## Shivangi Nadkarni, Co-founder and CEO, Arrka Consulting

Shivangi Nadkarni has over twenty-four years of experience in the domains of information risk, data privacy and networks. She handled multiple roles over the years at Sify and Wipro, before she co-founded Arrka Consulting. Arrka empowers organizations to implement and manage data privacy and security programmes via the Arrka Privacy Management platform. Shivangi has authored India's first textbook on data privacy for Data Security Council of India (DSCI) – a Nasscom body – for their DCPP (DSCI-Certified

Privacy Professional) programme. She is also a member of the world's largest privacy body – Asia Advisory Board of the IAPP (International Association of Privacy Professionals).

Shivangi holds a master's degree in management from IIM Calcutta and a bachelor's degree in Electrical and Electronics Engineering from BITS Pilani. She has also completed certification for many data privacy and security roles: Certified Information Systems Auditor (CISA) from Information Systems Audit and Control Association (ISACA); Certified Information Privacy Professional/IT (CIPT) from IAPP; DCPP from DSCI; and Certified Data Privacy Solution Engineer (CDPSE) from ISACA. A regular speaker at various forums, Shivangi also teaches advanced privacy courses to industry professionals.

## The Genesis of Arrka

SHIVANGI WAS AHEAD OF THE CURVE WHEN SHE CO-FOUNDED Arrka with Sameer Anja in 2012. The vision of the company was to equip enterprises with information risk, data privacy and cybersecurity management solutions.

Her decade-long stint with Sify, which began in 1996 – soon after she graduated from IIM Calcutta – gave her her first experience of working in the cybersecurity space. When the Information Technology Act, 2000, was passed in India, digital signatures issued by certifying authorities (CAs) became a reality in the country. At that juncture, Sify decided to tie up with VeriSign – then a global leader in the domain – to set up a CA in India and introduce digital signatures.

Shivangi was in charge of this project and helped set up Sify as India's first licensed CA, branded as SafeScrypt, under the new IT Act. Consequently, she built a data security business for the company with this at its core. This is essentially how she entered the world of encryption and security. Reminiscing about the early days in this domain, she says, 'I recently met one of our channel partners from my Sify days when we used to sell Secure Sockets Layer, or SSL, certificates. We would manage to sell one certificate in a month after visiting the client several times. Today, this channel partner tells me, he sells 150–200 certificates in a day.'

Post a successful run with Sify, Shivangi moved on to head Wipro's Global Identity & Application Security practice in 2006. While she enjoyed and learned a lot during the short one-and-a-half-year stint at Wipro, she soon realized that her heart was not in large organizations. 'Sify spoilt me by injecting an entrepreneurial mindset in my blood,' is how Shivangi describes things.

So she decided to strike out on her own. Her first two attempts were 'spectacular failures', as she puts it. Just as she was wondering whether she should go back to a regular, highly lucrative and well-paying corporate job, she met her current co-founder – Sameer Anja. Sameer had just quit KPMG and was starting out on his own too. The two decided to join forces and build something together in the infosec domain. This marked the beginning of Arrka.

## Consultancy to Data Privacy

In the early days of Arrka, the duo focussed on providing consultation in the infosec domain to primarily small and mid-sized companies. 'Organizations run by friends or acquaintances who called us to help them "sort out this security stuff",' as Shivangi puts it. Around the same time, she stumbled into the domain of data privacy. 'A senior colleague from the industry whom I highly respect, told me that I should check out data privacy as it is going to become big one day. I ended up taking a data privacy certification exam from the IAPP which was happening for the first time in India. And thus it all began.' Today, Shivangi serves on the Asia Advisory Board of the IAPP.

Soon after, Nasscom set up DSCI to focus on security and privacy challenges in the country and gave Arrka their first break in data privacy. Shivangi helped them design their first training programme – DSCI-Certified Privacy Lead Auditor (DCPLA – and she continues to serve as faculty for DSCI. Subsequently, she helped DSCI design a second privacy certification programme – DCPP – for which she authored the textbook as well. It is India's first textbook on data privacy.

## Data Privacy Laws

Though India doesn't have a data protection law yet, Shivangi believes it is only a matter of time. 'We are the world's second-largest digital nation after China. And the data of our citizens is available to the entire world to do almost whatever they want to with it. No other geography of comparable size and stature offers such a carte blanche!' She notes that the declaration of privacy as a fundamental right by the Supreme Court in 2017 was a game-changing development. 'When something is a fundamental right, essentially no law can be passed that contradicts or takes away or diminishes that right.' Explaining further developments in the matter, Shivangi says, 'Then the government constituted a commission under Justice B. N. Srikrishna to come up with a data privacy law. The commission first developed a framework that was put up for public comment and subsequently, based on that, the Personal Data Protection Bill (PDPB) was drafted.' A modified version of this bill was introduced in the Lok Sabha in December 2019. It was sent to a Joint Parliamentary Committee (JPC) for review. 'Given that the data of 1.2 billion people is at stake, the whole world is keenly waiting for this bill and the subsequent law.'

At the time of writing, the JPC's report is scheduled to be presented in Parliament during the 2021 monsoon session.

In Shivangi's opinion, what has set the data privacy ball really rolling – in an accelerated manner – is the passing of the General Data Protection Regulation (GDPR) by the European Union in 2016. It has given a major push to the rest of the world to reconsider personal data protection. 'Although Europe has always had privacy laws, GDPR was a significant amendment because it forced everyone to re-look at privacy and the protection of personal data "grounds up", keeping the current reality in mind. The kind of penalties that the GDPR talks about (2–4 percent of a company's global turnover) have made sure everyone sat up and took it very seriously. Subsequent to the GDPR, we are witnessing privacy laws along similar lines being passed by other countries around the world.'

## Walls Have Ears

Since the advent and growing popularity of voice-controlled smart devices, not to mention smartphones, there has been active concern around the lack of privacy that accompanies them. Shivangi explains, 'It's not just Amazon's Alexa and Google Home – more than 50 percent of our mobile apps have microphone and camera access. A couple of years ago, there was a case where the police requested to use the recordings made by Alexa for a murder investigation, but Amazon refused to give them up, saying it would be a violation of privacy. Whether this was the right call or not, one can't know for sure. The laws are still catching up and the world is still figuring things out. These are indeed very interesting times.'

Shivangi and the Arrka team keep a close track of relevant legal and regulatory changes in data privacy and align closely with policy folks as well. 'We are implementation specialists, so we help organizations implement privacy programmes, addressing whatever laws and regulations come their way. We help them manoeuvre the hurdles that come their way.'

## Women in the Workplace

Having grown up in a progressive household, Shivangi counts herself fortunate to never have faced gender discrimination. 'My parents treated me and my brother the same. Even during my time at BITS, gender discrimination was never really a point of discussion.'

Her own professional journey has been a relatively smooth one. 'As a woman in the corporate world for the last twenty-five years, I have personally never really faced the proverbial glass ceiling or other challenges. Having said that, not all women are as lucky. Rather, I am an exception. I have seen a lot of women leave their jobs because of lack of family support, women who end up taking on most of the burden of child-rearing, elder care and looking after other household chores instead.'

A woman of ideals, Shivangi does not hesitate to question unfair workplace behaviour. 'When I was working with Wipro, a colleague returning from her maternity leave wasn't considered for a project in Australia as the person in charge of allocation assumed she wouldn't take up the project, given that she had a four-month-old child at home. I told him that was unfair and called up my colleague to ask her whether she wanted to be a part of the project. She jumped at the opportunity, taking her mother and baby with her to Australia for six months to complete the project. People find ways to make things happen if they want to.'

Shivangi feels that senior women in the workforce can indeed do quite a bit to support other women and facilitate their climb up the corporate ladder. 'Mentoring goes a long way. I have been fortunate to have a lot of good mentors, and that has made all the difference.' With firms actively working towards including more women in the workforce, Shivangi is optimistic about the future of women in the corporate world.

## Go with the Flow

As someone who chooses to take a flexible and relaxed approach in both life and business, Shivangi points out that it is important to live in the present. 'Don't be too hard on yourself. You don't need to have strict deadlines to achieve your goals. The world is changing so fast that if you set rules, you block out opportunities. Instead, go with the flow. Make sure what you do challenges you. If you get up in the morning and have to think twice about why you're doing what you're doing, don't do it. Don't be scared of changing tracks. There's so much to learn from every interaction you have, every person you meet, every book you read. It's a whole wide world out there, and it's up to you to grab the opportunities that come your way.'

Shivangi thoroughly enjoys her area of work and even after a long day at work, she rarely feels stressed. 'But sometimes, it gets mentally exhausting as you are required to concentrate for long hours. I divide my day into phases to ensure I have enough breaks in between sessions that require a lot of focus.'

On a regular weekday after work, Shivangi likes to catch up on movies streaming on Netflix or pick up a book. And if she has a free weekend – which, according to her, does not happen very often in her line of work – she likes to travel.

## Back to BITS

Shivangi fondly remembers her days in the idyllic locale of Pilani as the best days of her life. Even three decades after graduation, she clearly remembers her college ID number – 88A3PS083. 'I think any BITSian would tell you the best four years of their life were the ones they spent in BITS. I went to IIM Calcutta after graduation, but the years I spent there don't compare to my time at BITS.'

She loved the quietude offered by Pilani's remote location with hardly any motor vehicles in sight. 'The only way anybody could contact you was via a trunk call – there was no STD either. There was one phone in the warden's room which you could use in case of an emergency, otherwise you could only rely on handwritten letters.'

Within the campus, she enjoyed hanging out with her friends in the Sky Lawns – a garden in front of the Birla Science Museum – which was one of the spots where students socialized. During a recent visit to the campus, she reconnected with Pappu, the owner of Sky Labs (a little shop at Sky Lawns). 'Pappu told us that students nowadays don't frequent his shop as much. They hang around there in between lectures or when they are hungry, but not as much as before. When we went there for our Silver Jubilee Meet, he gave free *shikanji* (lemonade) to everyone.' It has been quite some time since Shivangi graduated, yet any mention of her BITS days fills her with joy and nostalgia. 'BITS is magic. It changes you and defines you for life.'

# DIFFERENTIATE OR PERISH

## Sunil Duggal, Former CEO, Dabur India Ltd

Sunil graduated from BITS Pilani in 1979 with a bachelor's degree in Electrical and Electronics Engineering. He further pursued a career in management by joining IIM Calcutta, completing his postgraduation in 1981, which was when he joined Wimco as a management trainee. Sunil left Wimco in 1992 as the head of Sales and Marketing, after which he did a three-year stint at Pepsico India Holdings as All India Sales Operations Manager. Sunil joined Dabur India Ltd in 1995 as the general manager of Sales & Marketing and went on to become the firm's longest-serving CEO.

Sunil is also known to have given Dabur a new direction, turning it into one of the most valuable FMCG companies in India. Under his leadership, the company diversified its portfolio from traditional Ayurvedic products to fruit beverages and personal care products. He built Real into India's largest fruit juice brand and Dabur Red Toothpaste into India's third-largest toothpaste brand. He also oversaw successful acquisitions of four companies, two in India and two overseas and helped in formulating a very successful CSR agenda for Dabur aimed at alleviating hunger and malnutrition and plastic waste management. His work has earned him numerous accolades, such as being recognized as FMCG CEO of the Year thrice and as one of India's top wealth creators.

## Promoter to Professional

LIKE EVERY ESTABLISHED FIRM, DABUR HAS DEVELOPED ITS unique DNA over the several decades of its existence. In this respect, Sunil sees Dabur as an Ayurveda brand, and banking on Ayurveda products has worked well for the firm. 'We have tried to be unique in that approach, and not blindly imitating bigger multinationals has helped us get where we are today.' Dabur group was promoter-driven until 1998 but it moved towards a professionally run approach thereafter. 'Even though

I used to encourage promoters to take an active interest in the business, their involvement in the business was minimal.'

With Sunil at the helm, Dabur saw seventeen glorious years. During his tenure, the company's revenue, market cap and profit after tax jumped multifold and Dabur's global presence, too, increased to over 110 countries. Revenues grew from ₹1,264 crore to ₹8,533 crore and profit from ₹106 crore to ₹1,469 crore. 'Before 2002, we were among the top ten FMCG companies but today we are in the top five in India, in terms of revenue and profitability. We got Accenture to help us with strategic planning, and we put in the best-in-class processes that McKinsey & Co. had initiated. Their design to help us transition from promoter to professional was great but did have issues with execution. You see, consultants are great at planning but poor at operations.' Sunil's plan was clear. He wanted to set Dabur on the path to success and globalize the company by accelerating organically and inorganically through acquisitions in the domestic as well as international markets.

## International Markets

While on one of many business tours in Turkey, Sunil had suggested expanding Dabur's presence in the Middle East to his colleagues. 'After convincing others, we bought a firm called Hobi Kozmetik Group in Turkey. It has been doing stupendously well and has got a Compounded Annual Growth Rate (CAGR) of 20 percent. The risk in doing international business is that the currency can plummet, and it did in our case too. Turkish Liras plummeted from 31 units when we bought the firm to 12 units. The currency deprecating to half resulted in losses for a few years as we calculated our revenue in INR. The company has since begun to generate substantial profits.'

But Sunil doesn't regret his decision to expand, even though the currency fluctuations had set them back by a bit. 'The depreciating currency value was an external factor, one that no one considered. These are the pros and cons, and you have to deal with them. When you go overseas, you can either hit a jackpot or a pothole, but that doesn't mean you shouldn't do it, because even if the business doesn't do great, there is so much to learn.'

## Acquisitions: Domestic vs International

Acquisitions in India, according to Sunil, are an expensive affair – acquiring a company abroad typically costs half to one-third of what acquiring its Indian counterpart would do. He cautions against the common mistake of buying a company that is highly overvalued. For instance, Dabur has completed two important acquisitions – Balsara, an oral care portfolio, and Fem, a foray into skincare. Sunil believes these acquisitions were successful as Dabur was able to recognize the embedded value in these enterprises even though they were losing money. 'We knew with our team, capability and experience that we would gather immediate profit.'

Sunil remarks that although these acquisitions could have turned out to be costly, the risks associated with such ventures in India are much lower. A trick that has worked out for Sunil and Dabur in domestic acquisitions is appointing a senior executive as the mentor of the acquired company. The mentor oversees all business operations to make sure that the company doesn't get lost in the crowds. The executive comes back to their original position once the company accelerates and is settled.

When it comes to overseas acquisitions, Sunil advises being even more cautious and keeping in mind the political and economic risks. 'If I were to do an international acquisition now, I'd not prefer entering a new country. I wouldn't want that because it's a totally new environment and there are way too many variables to account for. While expanding internationally, we also ensured that both legs of the business ran almost independently. Both the supply chains were localized, and this helped us in the long term. Even financially, it turned out to be a prudent decision for us.'

## Urban vs Rural Consumers

Sunil feels that an average second-tier rural consumer is not too different from the average urban consumer. 'The rural consumer is far more value-conscious, buys smaller units at affordable price points and doesn't waver too much in terms of purchasing behaviour. The rural consumer wants the same shampoo as their urban counterpart, but instead of buying a bottle that will cost them ₹100 rupees, they will buy a

₹1 sachet, but it doesn't change the fact that the rural consumer is equally brand- and value-conscious,' explains Sunil, who encourages tapping into rural distribution networks to gain massive profits. The only difference, according to Sunil, lies in the consumption rate, which is lower in rural areas, but as affordability grows, so will consumption.

## Innovation and Tech

Sunil proudly shares, 'We were one of the earlier companies to adopt enterprise networks and were arguably the pioneers then. We began using analytics very early on, and our supply chain has been completely transformed through technology. There have been several business changes over the years. A recent one was GST, where we had to completely redesign our systems. However, one of our most important metrics that we kept a close eye on was "lost sales" due to supply chain failures. We are pretty obsessed with having minimum possible sales loss, especially because of the portfolio that we have in India. So technology has been absolutely pivotal for us. We used technology in our forecasting and that helped us stay one step ahead. But one should use technology as a tool or an enabler and not as something to be used just because everyone's doing it.'

## Marketing-wise

Sunil has spent years travelling within the country and abroad and claims that the best way to learn about one's consumers is to take a field trip, interact with the distributors, retailers and consumers, instead of doing market research and studying insights sitting in corporate offices. 'Marketing is the core of any company, and one should spend more time in the field instead of spending time with focus groups,' asserts Sunil. 'Market research, too, is helpful in some ways, but it isn't helpful in a holistic sense. Say for example, you have to decide between three variants of red toothpaste. The market research might indicate the winning variant, yet that wouldn't guarantee success. The whole lesson is "differentiate or perish". If you don't differentiate, then you won't flourish. Don't follow the leader, the leader will crush you. Try to carve your own path.'

## The Competition

Sunil feels secure about Dabur's future, based on how the firm has performed against its rivals in the past. Taking Patanjali's example, he says, 'Patanjali made promises which weren't fulfilled, but they did come very hard at us, taking away many shares in products like honey and toothpaste, but Dabur has fought back valiantly.' Sunil claims Dabur has stronger propositions, better supplies and better value in the eyes of the consumers in terms of sustainable quality. Our manufacturing and supply chains are very sophisticated, which Patanjali couldn't match. You can't do so much so quickly. In their case, the supply chain unravelled.'

## Dabur and Ayurveda

Brand-creation and distribution are equally expensive tasks, but investments made in both can be combined to form a reliable moat, says Sunil. 'The moat is strengthened when the products are highly differentiated and have high loyalties. When Dabur launched the red toothpaste, it really changed the rules of the game. We introduced the usage of red oxide, because we wanted to accentuate Dabur as a true Ayurvedic brand. We believed in this and knew that launching another Colgate wasn't going to be successful.' Today, Dabur is closing on ₹1000 crore on the red toothpaste; Sunil considers it to be one of the company's finest achievements.

Sunil is cognizant of Dabur's pole position in the Ayurvedic market. The Indian business ecosystem, he asserts, is a completely different ball game. 'In the past five years or so, I have realized that we have to go back to our roots and recreate the benefits of Ayurveda, especially in consumer healthcare. Consumers today prefer herbal alternatives, for which Dabur is their go-to choice.' He sees the rise of Baba Ramdev as a confirmation of his belief that Indians have a certain liking for traditional medicine. His suggestion is for Dabur to expand into other areas such as personal care, where Ayurveda isn't well established yet. 'Although I won't be able to complete this journey, I sincerely hope that my successors move Dabur's India portfolio towards the Ayurvedic space, and thereafter, focus on extending it overseas.'

## Challenges at the Helm

Sunil has witnessed Dabur grow multifold, but it has come at a cost. 'When your firm is listed, you have to answer to not just the board but also the promoters and the public. You have to publish the results every three months, in front of 500 people from all around the globe on a conference call, and that isn't easy. I had to do this sixty-four times in my career.' He also feels that emotional engagement causes and adds to the pressure as you begin to consider the efforts you are putting in for the company to make sure that you are an asset. 'It is stressful, and even though I loved this job, I didn't want it to burn me out. That is why choosing a successor is an integral part of the job,' says Sunil, weighing in his two cents. 'An insecure CEO is lethal for any company and is something no company should tolerate.'

## Dabur and Beyond

Having spent seventeen years as the CEO of Dabur and a total of twenty-four with the firm, Sunil has collected innumerable memorable moments from his professional career. A memory that stands out for him is from 2002 when, the then chairman of Dabur, Ashok C. Burman, had called him to his house. 'He wanted me to take over the firm,' says Sunil, who recalls being 'flabbergasted' by the proposition. 'The opportunity seemed quite transformative, and although I was thinking of other alternatives, I finally chose to step up and accept the new position as Dabur's CEO.' This was followed by a stellar career that has witnessed many milestones, acquisitions, successful overseas ventures; and it is achievements like these that reassure Sunil that he made the right decision back then.

'However, when I turned 60, I wished to leave Dabur, or at least be semi-retired. The promoters respected my decision but asked me to find my replacement. This took us another couple of years after a lot of back and forth, and we were able to finalize Mohit Malhotra as my successor. Planning this succession was one of the most important tasks for me. I have also laid down guidelines for the company to follow in the next decade.'

In his life's next chapter, Sunil wants to catch up on whatever he has missed out on during his professional life. He wants to spend more time with his family and travel around, but this time not for business. He doesn't want to bow out of public life completely either, rather he hopes to continue with the engagements he enjoys. 'I want to give back to the country and that's why I am interested in helping Indian brands and not the MNCs, as they have already got enough resources. I want to engage with a small Indian company instead. That's what the plan really is.'

## Back to BITS

Being a student at BITS, Sunil shares, helped his professional career as it offered a myriad of courses as part of a holistic curriculum. In his pre-final year, Sunil decided that he didn't want to pursue engineering any further. 'Honestly, I wasn't very good at it – there were many others who were academically better than me. I wanted to do something in management, and hence wanted to pursue an MBA from any of the top three IIMs.' Sunil never desired to travel overseas for an MBA, and was, in fact, delighted when he received an offer from IIM Calcutta. 'I put in a lot of hard work in my formative years, spending quite a few years on the ground and in sales, where I got the opportunity to learn the harsh reality and witness first-hand what India is about, and that lesson has always stuck with me.'

# BE FLEXIBLE

## T. P. Pratap, Co-founder, Qwikcilver Solutions

T. P. Pratap holds a bachelor's degree in Electronics and Electrical Engineering from BITS Pilani and an MBA from IIM Calcutta. Pratap is the co-founder of Qwikcilver Solutions, India's pioneering gift card technology product company responsible for establishing the gift card industry in the country. He is also the chief marketing officer of Woohoo, launched by Qwikcilver in 2015.

Prior to founding Qwikcilver, Pratap had worked in various corporate roles with leading corporations like Wipro, ICI, Timex and Kuwaiti Danish Dairy. When he is not evangelizing the resilient Indian startup ecosystem and the power of digital gifting to the world at large, Pratap strives to make himself useful at home to his entrepreneurial artist-wife and two children by harnessing his inadequate culinary skills.

## Creating a Market

PRATAP WAS SAILING INTO UNCHARTED TERRITORY WHEN HE conceptualized Qwikcilver along with Kumar Sudarsan and Bhaskar Vasudevan in 2006. This technology startup went on to pioneer a whole new gifting category in India and beyond. It has done so by building and scaling a full-stack, cloud-hosted SaaS platform. 'We were thankfully not aware of how challenging it was going to be when we started off! Changing consumer behaviour is challenging from a cultural and societal context. It requires immense passion, commitment and conviction over a long period of time to drive such a change,' explains Pratap.

'Gifting is a tricky business which brings into the picture even trickier human engagement. It's tough to find the right gift. You want to gift a shirt or a pair of shoes, but you can't seem to get the size right. On birthdays or weddings, out of the several gifts one receives, there are always overlaps. Sometimes, both the gifter and the receiver are not pleased with the outcome. This is where Qwikcilver comes into the picture.'

Qwikcilver started off as a pure play technology platform provider and over the years, has firmed its position in the gift card category space in India. It is the only end-to-end, fully integrated prepaid and gift card solutions provider in the country. 'Our Woohoo brand, launched in 2015, has grown to become the most preferred online destination for gift cards for Indian consumers and corporates, which give gifts to employees and dealers on various occasions like festivals or to reward professional performances. More than 70 percent of the gifting in rewards and recognition programme catalogues is preferred to be done through gift cards today.' Woohoo provides innovative personalized options for customers to choose from a wide range of brands and denominations. Pratap beams with pride as he says, 'We are indeed pleased that Qwikcilver and Woohoo have been showcased as a case study by *Harvard Business Review* and also at various technology and leading business schools.'

## The Qwik Way

Qwikcilver convinces well-established brands to partner with them and boasts of having clients across thirty countries. Elaborating on their method, Pratap explains, 'The first step toward a successful gift card transaction is landing a long-term partnership with a famous brand. It is also the toughest challenge because it takes a lot of concentrated effort to evangelize a firm and pitch gift cards as an alternate form of currency. It has to be tailor-made for their brand and mapped to suit their ecosystem. Once the brand sees gift cards as their personalized currency, they have a great time customizing them. Where, how and when one can use the card is solely the brand's call.' He also goes on to attribute their success to his team's dedicated focus and passion to build their business over the last decade to a great scale.

The company also makes it a point to make sure that their stored-value platform is safe and secure. 'We need to ensure that only the intended recipient has access to the gift card. It would be a fraud otherwise. At the same time, the concept of gifting via gift card has to be fun and vibrant for it to realize greater customer engagement for the brands.'

## Creating a Win-Win Scenario

Qwikcilver's business builds win-win partnerships for the long term. Pratap cites how each party in the partnership benefits from the association: 'A gift card, instead of just cash, is an asset for the partner brand because it drives additional revenue, increases footfall and boosts working capital and profits for the brand. The brand also gains two customers instead of one. The customer who purchases the card inadvertently vouches for the brand associated with it and gifts it to the person who will eventually avail it.'

Pratap believes that gift cards have opened new doors for a range of brands that were conventionally not thought of as gifting options. 'There are some brands which are ingrained in our minds as the ones that belong to the gifting segment, namely cookware, watches and clothing. Through cards, the gifting portfolios have significantly expanded. Otherwise, who would have thought of groceries, lingerie, holiday, air travel and salon appointments as a gifting option?' With nearly 90 percent of the gift card market share under its belt and having issued over 2 billion gift cards till date, Qwikcilver has raised funds from Amazon, Accel Partners and several other notable investors. When Pine Labs acquired Qwikcilver in 2019, the fantastic growth and performance of the company had enabled a stellar exit, making it one of the success stories of VC-funded Indian tech startups.

## Trusting Domestic Potential

When Pratap was starting out with Qwikcilver, many well-wishers and even his investors suggested that he focus on taking the business abroad. Even though the product was appreciated, they believed that the conditions in India were not conducive to the growth of a B2B platform due to certain restrictions like government red tape. But the co-founders thought differently. 'Our conviction that the Indian market has immense potential has been fruitful in the long term. The complexities of addressing the needs of consumers across Indian markets has also enabled us to build a robust technology platform.' Qwikcilver has expanded its business to the Middle East, Southeast Asia, Australia and, most recently, Europe.

In its early years, the company depended on loyalty programmes, a common preference of most brand owners in those days, but they realized there were a lot of other players in the same space. 'We were confident that we would be able to establish our place in the uncharted gift card market space and build a strong customer base. This foresight pointed us in the right direction, and we are now the most preferred gift card product suite for more than 2,500 enterprises and corporates.'

## Need for Frugality

'Right from the beginning, we have built Qwikcilver to scale effectively and profitably with judicious investments over time in strategically relevant functional areas. We believed that our business should stand on its own instead of solely depending on external funding. It's not to say that we've not raised money – we've raised money but the amounts we've raised do not commensurate with the scale we have achieved. This clarity of the cause has helped us consistently drive business goals and address our customer requirements.'

Pratap recommends frugality in business. 'Building big consumer startups does require immense investments and a cash-intensive strategic voyage. For a startup, raising funds is important, but how much, when, how to use it and for what purposes, are critical decisions that eventually determine its fate. A cookie can crumble, and it has crumbled for large entities who raised big money. One needs to understand that even the investors have to show returns, hence it's important to evaluate the implications and potential outcomes before raising money for your venture.'

## Marketing Lessons

'Possessing strong domain knowledge across the market and its different segments is of utmost value in marketing any product. Today, opportunities and information are more accessible than ever before, but that also makes understanding the nuances of the business from the customer's perspective a demanding task.' Pratap considers customization to be a formidable challenge too, because every Indian firm wants the product to be tailor-made for them, and the process of customization is a 'draining' one. Ideally, a product should be built in a way that while its functioning remains the same at its core, it can be deployed for any brand. 'There is no one-size-fits-all strategy or the right time to market a SaaS product. It's best to go out there, build and enhance the platform as you go along. The domain knowledge would be relevant in scaling the product over its life cycle.'

## No Shortcuts

An optimistic Pratap suggests that there are enough opportunities in today's market and enough customer problems that need to be catered to. 'BITSians can do it,' remarks Pratap enthusiastically. 'Don't worry too much about the naysayers or even funding! There are no shortcuts in the entrepreneurial world. There are some glamorous stories, but they don't show how much hard work has gone into making a company successful.' To the ones setting out on their entrepreneurial journey, Pratap advises to be wary of failures, but never be bogged down by them. 'Being emotionally attached to your product or company won't do you any good. Sometimes, things don't work out and you have to let them go. Be prepared for that, be flexible.'

Scaling a business is a joint effort, attests Pratap. 'As a founder, you cannot do everything by yourself. A successful venture is built by the efforts and strength of a capable leadership team. We have had some fantastic colleagues who have been there with us through tough times. Having a passionate team with the required skills and the confidence to work for the long haul makes all the difference.'

## Back to BITS

Pratap's memories of BITS remain fresh to this day, even though he graduated in 1991. He looks back at his college days with nostalgia and says that he appreciates the time spent in BITS now, but remembers campus life at Pilani as being difficult when he was a student. 'There were some great parts – wingies, friends, fests, clubs and departments, bunking classes, going to C'not and Sky Lawns. But Pilani's isolated location meant I, along with most students, couldn't travel home as often as we'd like.' Apart from the homesickness, Pratap and his batchmates complained about the mess food, the bitter winter chill and the boiling summer heat. 'Back in the day, we could be in touch with our families only through letters, which were delivered once in two weeks. Although being away from family and urban life was tough, it made us self-sufficient.'

In hindsight, Pratap considers the remote location and zero-attendance policy to be a blessing in disguise, as it helped him bond better with his batchmates. 'There were no city-life distractions. You met groups of people, bonded with them, had a good time, and that became your college life. All this bonding was catalyzed by non-scholastic activities, especially working together for college fests, which are run entirely by student organizations. We bonded closely over the tough winds that blew across the dunes!'

He considers himself lucky to have studied with a diverse group of capable individuals, which provided him with a great deal of exposure early on. He admits, 'Adapting and adjusting to Hindi, Tamil and Telugu was quite eye-opening. I am glad that I learnt so many languages while marooned in the desert! A tiny, scrawny version of me also bravely ventured for the first time into the gym to work out with my regular, beefier batchmates.'

Pratap remains eternally grateful to his alma mater at '333031' (the PIN code of Pilani) for imbuing in him the confidence to take on the hardest of life's challenges.

# LEARNING NEVER STOPS

## Tulsi Mirchandaney, MD, Blue Dart Aviation

Tulsi Nowlakha Mirchandaney is the managing director and the accountable manager at Blue Dart Aviation, India's first and only scheduled domestic cargo airline, with a fleet of six Boeing 757 freighters. She is responsible for the organization's flight and ground operations, in-house security, airframe line and heavy maintenance. During her tenure, the company expanded its capacity by phasing out the classic B737-200 freighters and replacing them with the more fuel-efficient B757 freighters. She has been instrumental in expanding the company's infrastructure across airports. She played a critical role in bringing about policy changes in civil aviation to highlight the significance of air express and ensuring the sustainability of the cargo airline industry in the country. She has been actively associated with the airline and express industry in India for over fifty years and with the Blue Dart group for twenty-five years. She was also involved in the launch of Blue Dart Aviation prior to its inception in 1996.

Tulsi is the co-chair of the Confederation of Indian Industry's (CII) National Committee for Civil Aviation for 2019–20 and 2020–21. She has an MBA in International Aviation from Concordia University, Montreal, and has been felicitated by the Ministry of Civil Aviation for her contribution to civil aviation in the country.

## Women in the Workplace

TULSI MIRCHANDANEY CONSIDERS HERSELF FORTUNATE TO have been brought up with her two brothers as equals. 'In Shillong, my brothers and I went fishing and shooting together. It was only when I arrived in north India that I first noticed the cultural gender divide. It was my first encounter with the reality of an unfair world and the portent of future challenges.'

So when she was inducted into the cargo segment of an airline, a traditionally male-dominated field, she had already been apprised of the challenges ahead. 'When I started my career in air cargo, we were referred to as the "Backroom Boys", because we were relegated to the less glamorous entrails of the aircraft,' chuckles Tulsi, explaining that even though cargo isn't the most alluring side of the business, it is just as, if not more, critical than the passenger segment of the airline.

'Cargo was then more profitable than the passenger side of the business. It brought incremental revenue at low cost, with the flexibility of optimizing the aircraft capacity,' she explains. At the time, she was often the only woman at the various meetings she attended. In time, her industry colleagues and customers got used to her presence and active involvement in the field. 'It did not matter because, in the end, your value is determined by your actions and what you contribute.' With experience, Tulsi realized that the most demanding task in an organization is dealing with people. If you can master the art of communication and response, you provide perspective to your position. 'You can't control every situation, but you can certainly control your reaction.'

## Path to Being an MD

Tracing her journey to the top, Tulsi recounts, 'I joined the airlines to fund my future education, but the allure of aviation reset all my plans. I climbed up the ranks with the knowledge I gained from tackling unanticipated, adverse situations and accepting diverse roles across the country.' She sees mentors as the 'unsung heroes' of any organization and mentions having learned a great deal from her own mentors, who were excellent professionals and experts in their respective domains. 'A lot of what I am today, I owe to their generosity of spirit in sharing their expertise.'

'In 1995, one of the three founders of Blue Dart and a former industry colleague during my stint in Mumbai in the early 1980s, offered me a dream job, which I accepted with alacrity. When my journey with Blue Dart began, the shift to creating a structured, scheduled domestic cargo airline entailed a steep learning curve. The launch of India's first domestic cargo airline on 17 June 1996 across the five major airports of Chennai, Bangalore, Mumbai, Delhi and Kolkata, was a historic high, not just a milestone in the country's aviation history, but a memory cherished forever by all of us who had the privilege to be part of the project team. Twenty-five years on, Blue Dart Aviation is still charting new frontiers across Indian skies and, more recently, venturing beyond our boundaries. I feel so proud to be a catalyst for this journey with an organization that has changed the course of my life forever.'

Her work through the years eventually paved the way to the top for her, and she took charge as the managing director of Blue Dart Aviation in 2008.

Being the first cargo airline came with its own set of challenges, as the segment, though widely different, was inevitably clubbed with the passenger airlines when it came to framing policy. It was an uphill task, but was delighted to see the inclusion of Blue Dart's recommendations in the National Civil Aviation Policy of 2016, and the acknowledgement of air cargo and air express as an important sector in supporting the nation's economy. Her contributions have not just been restricted to her own organization, but have benefited the air cargo industry.

## The Future of Cargo

'Since its inception, Blue Dart Aviation made a strategic decision to control its service quality and invested in its human resources and assets to set up its own engineering line and airframe heavy maintenance, self-ground handling and security operations. While most airlines outsource their airframe heavy checks and ground handling, our professional team handles these tasks in-house. The reliability, speed, security and advanced technology delivery is intrinsic to the operations of Blue Dart Express, our parent company and leader in domestic air express. The past two decades have seen a graveyard of eight failed cargo airlines, most within six months of startup, which is a testimony to the arduous environment in which we operate. It is, therefore, important to establish the service-value equation. Our safety, on-time performance and technical dispatch reliability are drivers that help deliver the customer promise,' explains Tulsi.

'Nothing has highlighted the criticality of air cargo more strongly than the recent pandemic where air cargo played a stellar role. Under extremely difficult conditions, when most were confined to the safety of their homes, this segment of aviation worked every single day through the lockdown to provide the only accessible logistics network across the country and overseas. When the world stopped, we moved, bringing in essential supplies from across our borders.

'With its strategic location, large geography and manufacturing potential, India is ideally positioned to develop itself into an important regional hub.'

## Business by the Book

'*Atlas Shrugged*,' says Tulsi instantly, when asked about her favourite book. She describes this Ayn Rand classic as a pivotal piece of literature that changed her thinking during her impressionable teenage years. The favoured left-leaning ideology of those years (and there could be arguments on both sides) soon gave way to a different worldview. Aldous Huxley's *Brave New World* and George Orwell's *1984* are the other two books that take the top spots as her most inspirational. 'Both these books are spot on in their foresight and the authors have insightfully gauged the direction in which the world is headed. These three books impressed me because they were ahead of their time. Beyond their cynicism is an underlying message of human morality which seems to be dwindling today.'

She firmly endorses the view, in consonance with her organization's practice, that business ethics are crucial to the moral fibre of our society, and that there is an urgent need to encourage organizations to include care for their community and the environment, while running profitable businesses.

## Learning Never Stops

Tulsi remembers her days at Concordia University fondly, though waiting at bus stops in the icy winter, she often wondered what she was doing 'freezing to death in a foreign land'. She describes the journey of receiving her aviation degree as a tremendous experience. 'We were incredibly fortunate to have a fine faculty that consisted of experts working in the aviation industry and lecturers from MIT, among others. The faculty set a benchmark and helped us rise beyond our capabilities to push us to our highest potential.'

She lives by the motto 'learning never stops'. She enjoys attending summer school and amongst her interests is modern architecture. 'There's so much one can learn and there's so much being taught every day that one knows nothing about.'

Self-admittedly 'terrible' at assessing profitable investments for herself, Tulsi shares that she prefers investing in ideas through other means. 'There will be some who will accomplish what we may never achieve, however hard we strive. I feel the need to enable others to realize their potential and have set up a small annual endowment to this end, in the hope that a creative idea can see the light of day.'

## Work-Life Balance

'If you really want something and think that it will add value to your life, you should pursue it untiringly. Paths to your goal will emerge,' remarks Tulsi, her voice unwavering. When she went back to work four weeks after her son was born, it was difficult, but she realizes that adjusting to these new circumstances helped her organize and delegate work better. To women who have to juggle both professional and familial responsibilities, Tulsi's advice is to use their time wisely and accept that there will be changes along the way. Getting out of one's comfort zone is the best way to realize one's potential.

'Just gear up and tell yourself, "This is what I want to do. And maybe I'll sleep one hour less or maybe I won't have time to do a lot of things I like to do." Be prepared to make adjustments and compromises. As Ayn Rand says, there's no such thing as a sacrifice. Sacrifice is giving up something better for something worse. It's never a sacrifice if you're doing something to better yourself. Sometimes, you just need to be a better negotiator.'

## Valued Traits

Tulsi credits her professional success to one crucial quality: her unwavering focus. 'Focus makes everything else fall in line. While you need to have the humility to continuously re-educate yourself, a focused mind is what helps you achieve it. It helps you persevere and keeps you disciplined.' She also cautions against compromising on the quality of work. 'Entrepreneurs tend to fixate on getting things done, which may consequently affect the quality of execution.' When it comes to Indian businesses, she believes we can improve the execution of ideas and maintain global standards if we bridge the quality gap.

'If you love what you do, it brings joy, pride and a sense of purpose. This feeling of pride and purpose in employees is what separates a great firm from a good firm,' asserts Tulsi.

'Our values are central to our persona. Yet, as mere mortals, we are not infallible and we sometimes fall, regardless of our best intentions. What's important is that we rise again, be honest in recognizing our mistakes and resolve for them to never recur. Honesty builds the courage to tackle failure.'

## Back to BITS

When Tulsi joined BITS Pilani in 1967, she was 'awestruck' by how beautiful the campus was. 'I come from the North East with its lush green landscape, so entering a barren topography was a bit startling till I came across this oasis in the middle of the desert.' She was impressed by the infrastructure which she thought was ahead of its time. 'Both my brothers are IIT Kharagpur alumni. When I visited their campus, I realized that BITS was at par in terms of infrastructure, or even better,' shares a proud Tulsi.

On the other hand, the skewed gender ratio, not surprising for those times, was unsettling – more so the restrictions on female students' attire, diet and hostel timings. 'Meera Bhawan or MB, the girls' hostel, was like a fortress and perhaps rightly so, given the environment and sensibilities of the time. As a rebellious teenager, I was resentful. I'm sure it has undergone a sea change today, with women breaking through former all-male bastions in large numbers, slowly but surely, especially over the past two decades. I must admit that I found the facilities excellent and some of the faculty admirable and inspiring'. She eventually left the college to pursue her own path.

But looking back, she feels BITS taught her some important lessons for life. 'At a very young age, my experience at BITS taught me how to hold my ground, to strengthen and maintain my individuality, and to be an independent thinker.' She continues being in touch with some of her classmates and seniors from her college days. For her, BITS was a diverse haven that offered an opportunity to its students from all parts of the country to intermingle and share ideas in a world-class institution. 'Such an experience really opens your eyes,' concludes a reminiscent Tulsi.

# NO REGRETS

## Vinod Saraf, Founder and Executive Chairman, Vinati Organics Ltd

Vinod Saraf is the chairman of Vinati Organics – the largest manufacturer of ATBS and IBB in the world with more than 65 percent global market share and the largest manufacturer of IB and HP-MTBE in India. It has a market capitalization of over ₹11,000 crore and has multiplied shareholder wealth by a whopping 119 times over the past decade. Vinod's emphasis on clean and green technologies and their assimilation into his business earned Vinati Organics the EcoVadis' Gold Rating for sustainable performance. The recognition is bestowed only to the top 2 percentile companies out of over the 40,000 under consideration.

He was named the Business Leader of the Year (Innovation) by CHEMTECH CEW Leadership & Excellence Awards in 2011. He also shared the Dr P. C. Ray Award given to him by the Indian Chemical Council with National Chemical Laboratory (NCL) for commercializing indigenous technology for manufacturing ATBS in 2010.

## Going for Gold

IT'S COMMON KNOWLEDGE FOR THE ONES WHO ARE EVEN remotely acquainted with Vinod that he never requires a calculator for arithmetic – a skill he owes to his grandfather, who asked him mental math questions as a kid. Delving into his childhood, Vinod shares, 'Growing up in a small town, my primary school was in a *gurukul* setting. I started solving these arithmetic problems when I was quite young. I passed the fifth grade when I was just eight.' As Vinod gradually developed an interest in math, his grandfather made it clear that he didn't want Vinod to be a doctor or an engineer, and instead encouraged him to use his instincts and eventually run his own business. 'So I studied BCom and went on to become a gold medallist at Rajasthan University. A neighbour suggested that I pursue an MBA at BITS Pilani – one of few places in India where such a thing was being offered at the time. My batch was the fourth one to graduate with an MBA from BITS,' remembers Vinod.

The admission process used to be significantly different from undergraduate courses for MBA. A professor of business administration interviewed Vinod and selected him. He was the only commerce student in a batch of twenty MBA students that year. 'My commerce background gave me an edge in courses such as economics, management accounting, taxation and quantitative methods. I secured the G. D. Birla gold medal for academic excellence.' Vinod belonged to a humble background and takes great pride in the fact that he paid for his education through the scholarships he bagged in college.

## My Chemical Romance

Since Vinod had done his schooling at a Hindi-medium school, verbal English did not come very easily to him. As a result, he couldn't clear the vivas for MNCs like Hindustan Unilever. 'Post BITS, I took up a job in a spinning and weaving company in Bhilwara in Rajasthan, owned by Mr Jhunjhunwala. The interviewer had hired me after looking at my gold medals. Coincidentally, he was also a gold medallist from Presidency College.' Vinod was assigned to manage the LNG Bhilwara Group's newest factory for the next five years, after which his manager, Mr Hari Singh Ranka, set out to start his own venture in textiles and invited Vinod to join him. 'On joining his business, I realized that the textile business is extremely competitive. I worked there for over seven years and was the president of the company by the time I left it to join the Aditya Birla Group.'

'Sometime in 1988, when Hindustan Petroleum was looking for a joint sector partner for one of their refineries, I met them behalf of the Birlas and we were selected. I was made MD (Finance and Administration) of the company. Though this project never took shape, I came across a French petrochemical organization called the French Institute of Petroleum (IFP Energies) around that time. They developed technologies for manufacturing chemicals and had recently developed a method to manufacture isobutylbenzene (IBB) – an important intermediate to produce ibuprofen. IBB used to be an imported product but I conceived the idea in 1989 that we should manufacture it in India. What worked for us was that importing back in the 1990s was painful, and we could actually manufacture the intermediate here in India and supply to many ibuprofen manufacturers in Hyderabad and other places, such as Ahmednagar and Dombivali, and get them to stop importing IBB.' After Vinod procured the funding for this relatively expensive project, he got hold of a joint sector partner, Maharashtra Petrochemical Corporation Ltd, with MPCL having 26 percent equity and that's how Vinati Organics was born.

Vinati Organics had a tie-up with IFP, ensuring exclusive rights to their technology for producing IBB for seven years. 'Naturally, it increased our costs, but since this was a scarce technology then, this very expensive deal was justified. IFP, being a reputed firm, guaranteed the product's quality and the capacity of the plant. Moreover, having such a reliable partner helped us along the way.'

Vinod has been working since the age of nineteen, primarily in the textile and chemical sectors. 'The problem with textile is that you do double the work for half the pay. One of the most important things to keep in mind when you research a field is to check if there are any barriers to entry. If you are choosing the chemicals industry, look for these criteria – a globally competitive product, a niche chemical and a green method of production. The thing with textiles is that there is no complicated technology at work, you could simply install your own spinning mill. But in the chemical sector, you have complex requirements such as catalysts, without which you cannot carry out the production.'

## R&D for Success

Vinod had begun setting up his plant in 1989, and started working there on 11 December 1990, the day after quitting his job with the Birlas. 'Building the plant was a challenge, but it was a smooth ride after that. Once the plant was up and running, I started some projects that could integrate well with our setup and give us new lines of business. Just looking at the demand and supply of a product gives you only half the picture, it is the integration that ensures profitability. The only problem with this is that each project becomes time-consuming.' To save time and effort, Vinod suggested carrying out a thorough R&D exercise in-house. This led to partnerships with government labs like the NCL in Pune and the Indian Institute of Chemical Technology (IICT) in Hyderabad.

Vinod believes that India has abundant brainpower and corporates should come forward to sponsor research, develop new technology, help in setting up a pilot lab and further a commercial version if the opportunity is viable. 'One such promising product that came out of our research with NCL is 2-acrylamido-2-methylpropane sulfonic acid, or ATBS. Our primary product, IBB, is only used in ibuprofen, which is a mature market. ATBS can be used in water treatment, oil field chemicals, construction chemicals and paint emulsifiers. It took about four years to take off, and there was significant cash loss in the initial stages, but because IBB was doing so well, it more than covered up for the losses.'

When selecting chemical processes and products, Vinod goes for the ones that have long-term demand and are commercially attractive. He also prefers concentrating on core competencies to diversifying into other alien fields. A globally competitive niche product with a technological barrier remains his primary choice for his business and, at the same time, he is very mindful of its environmental impact.

## Family Business Dynamics

Vinod's family is actively involved in his business and has helped take a considerable load off his shoulders. 'My youngest brother Sunil and my children Vinati and Viral work with me. The credit for solving the ATBS problem and securing the agreement with the German company BASF goes to Vinati.' Vinati, a Wharton graduate, joined the family business in 2006. With her help and knowledge, they were able to find an experienced consultant from the US (an ex-Lubrizol scientist). 'He fixed the problems we were having with the plant and this stopped the cash loss for ATBS, and today, it is our primary product.

'After Vinati joined, there was a lot of growth in the company but work never spilled over into the household. One needn't work round-the-clock in the chemical industry, as it is a process-based industry.' Vinod comments that once the process has been set up, everything else is a cakewalk. 'I call the people at the factory in the morning for status updates. Vinati and I commute to the plant together, if we need to discuss anything with our employees.'

## An Effective Manager

Arithmetic calculations and a good memory have helped Vinod sail through his professional career. 'I am extremely satisfied with the education I received, and I have been proud of my career. I became a managing director at the age of thirty-eight. Luckily, my business worked out too. You need analytical skills to make good decisions and my MBA education helped accentuate my analytical power.'

Even though Vinod came from a commerce background, he knew it was critical for him to be aware of the technical details of each and every chemical being produced by his firm. 'If I didn't know these details, the technical people wouldn't let me be. To become an effective manager, you should know your product inside out.' Apart from this, having a strong hold over decision-making, analytical thinking, costing, budgeting and planning has aided him in becoming a better leader. He feels he has gotten better at selecting projects, which is the key to Vinati Organics' successful foray into a diverse range of chemicals.

'I have learnt a lot from my mentors Mr Jhunjhunwala and Mr Ranka. They taught me how to be a good administrator, how to manage a factory, and how to achieve targets. Working for the Birlas gave me good exposure, especially to the chemical industry, as I had the opportunity to study a lot of projects there.'

## Being Your Own Boss

Vinod has never been one to regret his decisions. When he quit his job in 1990, a lot of people were puzzled by his decision as he held a well-respected post as the managing director of the Mangalore Refinery & Petrochemicals Ltd (MRPL). 'I never saw quitting my job to start my own business as a risk. It looked like a lucrative project to me and I seized that opportunity. I had to do the same work at Vinati Organics which I was doing earlier, but I work for myself here.' Vinod took big projects and some hefty loans to support them too. 'The benefit of working for yourself is that you can make bolder decisions. You needn't justify your actions to anyone else, because the money you're risking is your own. I feel the second and third generations are more cautious, because they are reluctant to risk their existing wealth – a sentiment lacking in a first-generation entrepreneur.'

## Back to BITS

Vinod admits to never having been tech-savvy. 'I don't prefer using a computer. The first time I saw a computer was at Pilani – an IBM 1401. It was as big as a wardrobe, there was a card that had to be punched in Fortran IV. As an MBA student, I had access to the computer, but didn't quite enjoy using it.' A 1971 graduate, Vinod remembers his time at the college hostel clearly. 'I lived in Malviya Bhawan for both the years of my MBA – I can even tell you my room number. We shared a mess with Ram and Budh Bhawan. Most postgraduate and doctoral students were in my bhawan, and the undergrads lived in other bhawans.'

# YOU OWN YOUR CAREER

## V. T. Bharadwaj, Co-founder and General Partner, A91 Partners

V. T. Bharadwaj is a general partner at A91 Partners, an Indian private investment firm that seeks to partner with founders to build enduring businesses for tomorrow's India.

Before co-founding A91 Partners, V. T. was an MD at Sequoia Capital, a global venture capital firm in India, where he led investments in consumer, pharmaceutical and healthcare sectors. Prior to that, he worked at McKinsey & Co. He has an MBA from IIM Ahmedabad and a BE (Honours) in Electrical and Electronics Engineering from BITS Pilani.

V. T. is a trustee at Ashoka University, a board member of IIM Ahmedabad Endowment Management Company, a founding circle member of Museum of Art & Photography. He is also involved with Cuddles Foundation and Swasth Foundation.

## Consultant vs Venture Capitalist

FOR MANY WHO KNOW V. T., HIS MOST STRIKING FEATURE IS the red *tika* he sports with pride on his forehead. Though he has worked at several global organizations, such as McKinsey and Sequoia Capital, he does not remember being questioned about it in any of his professional interactions. But the tika has been at the centre of some funny misunderstandings. Once on a train in Germany, recollects V. T., someone assumed that his head was bleeding, only to discover that it was vermillion. Explaining its significance in his life, he says, 'This tika is a part of me in terms of who I am.' He believes in being comfortable in one's skin and never shying away from expressing oneself.

With six years as a consultant and twice as many as a venture capitalist under his belt, V. T. brings with him to the table, the experience of and expertise in both domains. 'Both are very different roles. Working with McKinsey, I realized consulting is about building solutions for the clients and their problems and enjoying the problem-solving process. At Sequoia, investing, for me, is about identifying great entrepreneurs, founders and opportunities and ascribing value to them. One needs to visualize the future of any opportunity five years down the line, while consistently helping entrepreneurs realize the value in the prospect.'

His role as a general partner at A91 Partners made V. T. realize that a fundamental part of the job is to empathize with investors and build a client base. 'They are the ones supporting the aspirations that you and your team have.' Both consulting and investing are apprenticeship businesses. It takes time to learn the ins and outs of the two, and they are different professional paths.

## Studying the Market

'At A91, we invest in companies that have scaled themselves up to ensure that the product-market fit is established. An idea becomes a business, and we invest in it to make it an enduring one,' says V. T., who places immense trust in his firm's modus operandi. He feels it is critical for an economist, or anyone intending to assess the market, to religiously read newspapers. 'The goal is to read in-depth reports about specific markets, interact with founders and their customers to get a sense of any behavioural change.' He feels reading such reports alerts one about new activities or changes in a specific domain. And it is equally important to identify whether the activity spawned from the domain itself or from the customer. 'Most insights come from our meetings with entrepreneurs. From the agreements and the disagreements therein, we devise our plan of action.'

## Creating a Moat

V. T. believes that without a real moat, there is no enduring business to be built. 'What you will have is a flash-in-the-pan acceleration of revenues that inspires innumerable copycats but no eventual profits. The challenge in any investment process is to find a competitive advantage in a business that makes it more sustainable.' He explains that an economic moat refers to a business's ability to maintain an advantage over its competitors, which offers protection of long-term profits and market shares. V. T. feels that in a consumer business, it is often easier to define a moat. 'For example, the reason that the distribution of your product is a moat is that it is not easy to get your product viably across multiple channels to all the customers in a large and complex market like India.'

With growing scale and depth, it becomes harder to enter and tap into the market that a business has created. 'You have to also keep in mind what the brand is promising, in terms of product and quality in consumer products. This is important, especially in a low-trust society like India, which is more starved for brands than markets. Here, the brand becomes a powerful moat because, time and again, people get cheated through fake products and claims. However, even brand value may erode with time, and hence, the next moat that companies usually build is a distributed manufacturing setup, much like one of our previous portfolio companies in the snacking space has done.' According to him, a distributed manufacturing setup helps in optimizing costs and thus becomes a moat in the longer run.

## A91 and Sugar

In January 2019, A91 led a ₹70-crore round in Sugar Cosmetics, their first investment and has been backing them since. V. T. is all praises for the company and its co-founders, Vineeta Singh and Kaushik Mukherjee (also BITS Pilani alumni). 'They showed phenomenal hustle and courage in building the business. We were extremely impressed with what they had achieved. With the advent of Jio in India, the internet became affordable and suddenly, it was possible for the current generation of Indian women to access makeup tutorials online.' Category creation, in V. T.'s opinion, is 'very hard' if the customer has to be taught from scratch, how to use the product. 'Today you have a culture where it is important to look good all through the day because you are constantly documenting your life through photographs. That's an example of a disruption caused by external factors. The target demographic being well-to-do women with disposable income. The make-up category has become more attractive for the investors.'

## Company Culture

In the story behind A91's name lies the vision of its founders for the company. V. T. explains, 'The A stands for Ashoka, an inspiration for excellence, ambition and humility, and 91 is a reference to 1991 – the year of economic reforms. I, along with two of my partners, wanted this firm to be an excellent Indian firm in its field. Hence the nomenclature.'

V. T. believes that a company's work culture must be consistent with its strategy. Culture-strategy incoherence creates conflict and disappointment, hampering the organization's success. This coherence must be ensured in every aspect of the organization. He elucidates this with an example. 'Let's say your company has a participative culture and believes that good decisions are taken when multiple individuals are involved in the brainstorming. This must reflect in your recruitment process as well. You must hire recruits who challenge you, because that's a part of constructive criticism.'

When it comes to collective contribution, he trusts in the power of discussion forums. 'People should be free to discuss and brainstorm, but they should also be fine with the organization not going forth with their opinion.' That, according to V. T., is the recipe for success and a healthy company culture.

## Bits of Wisdom

'We pass up too many opportunities in life, only to regret them later,' says V. T. as he tells us about the annual list he makes of interesting companies that he missed investing in, which eventually became incredibly valuable. 'I missed out on investing in Veeba Foods, which is an interesting company that makes sauces and spreads. There are way too many misses and mistakes in the investment arena. At the same time, he asserts the importance of not crying over spilt milk. 'It only makes you humbler. The key is to draw the right lesson from every experience and look ahead. Even this notion of making an annual balance sheet of "mistakes" on key decisions taken, is something I learned from an entrepreneur who has never raised capital to build his business.'

'*You* own your career, and only you get to decide what you want to do and become. Do not expect organizations to do it for you. You might be a part of the organization, but they have no responsibility in directing your career. It's your life,' states V. T. firmly.

He also emphasizes on the importance of having mentors and cordial professional relationships and shares that the most important takeaway is the set of relationships one builds in their organization. 'You may not always be a part of the same firm, but those relationships will continue to mean a lot.' On a sentimental note, V. T. says, 'It's very hard to know what truly makes you content. I suggest you take your time to discover that chance of finding true contentment in your work. In my experience, contentment at work is the ability to offer attention to what you are doing, without feeling the urge to look away. To paraphrase something I read recently, which I thought was quite fitting – true attention is, after all, the very definition of prayer, and work that inspires prayer has the chance to offer contentment.'

## Back to BITS

The 'most phenomenal thing' about BITS, according to V. T., was the respect the administration gave to the students in the form of complete autonomy to make fundamental decisions.

'They treated us like adults. How we wanted to manage our academic and co-scholastic life was completely our own decision, in terms of what courses we wanted to sign up for and what classes we wanted to attend. We were in the driving seat. In most of the classes I attended, I was sitting on the floor!'

V. T. was 'astonished' by the way the BITS administration functioned. He remembers it as being extremely understanding when there was a delay in transferring his admission fee. 'Imagine this happening to me while taking admission in a government college. But I met Dr Raghurama – then a professor in the Electronics and Instrumentation Department at BITS – and he told me not to worry. I was admitted as a late registrant, which meant I would be able to choose my courses in a slot scheduled a bit later, but the rest would remain the same. I could attend lectures like any other student.' V. T. feels there aren't many institutions that treat their students with such high regard and dignity.

# ACKNOWLEDGEMENTS

WE WOULD LIKE TO EXPRESS OUR SINCERE GRATITUDE TO THE following people who have made this book possible.

First and foremost, the twenty-five stellar BITSians who were kind enough to agree to the requests of two twenty-three-year-olds, who sought their time to interview them about their journeys, and for trusting us to document their lives.

To our parents, Poonam and Kawal Jit Sethi, and Neeta and Dr Rajendra Mandlecha, for their sacrifices to give us a holistic upbringing and always providing us with the best environment and resources to help us grow as individuals. Heartfelt gratitude to Durjai's aunt Manisha Sethi and his grandparents – Phoola Rani and her late husband Peshouri Singh Sethi, and late Usha Chandna and late Yash Pal Chandna – for their eternal and unconditional love and support. A special thanks to Gaurav's sister Khushboo Mandlecha for being a constant source of encouragement and sponsoring our US trips and multiple flights for the interviews.

To Kiran Nahata and Neena Nahata, Gaurav's uncle and aunt, who love him like their own son. Throughout the process of writing *The Pilani Pioneers* – while he stayed with them in Mumbai, juggling his day job at Viacom18 – they provided him with utmost comfort, joy and freedom so that we could focus on our dream of writing a book.

To the Mandlecha family back in Nashik: Satish Uncle, Santosh Uncle, Manoj Uncle, Rajashree Aunty, Smita Aunty, Rani Aunty and Gaurav's cousins – Saurabh, Pranav, Preksha, Kshipra, Kinjal and Arnav – who believed that we could pull off this audacious project.

To our dearest editors, Teesta Guha Sarkar and Elizabeth James at Pan Macmillan India, for their belief in the book and their faith in us. Thank you for lending your time and expertise, without which this book wouldn't have been as impactful. We grew stronger together and found friends in one another during the pandemic.

To Dilip D'Souza, celebrated writer and journalist and a fellow BITSian who was incredibly kind to introduce us first-time authors to Teesta. Without Dilip's support, this book wouldn't have found its home.

To Nandini Khanna and Nandini Tripathi, who have been pillars of strength throughout this odyssey. We are indebted to you for your thoughts, opinions and support, which helped shape the book. To our closest friends, Samarth Shah, Saurabh Shetty, Reehan Shah, Akul Goutham, Salvi Singh, Vidhi Shah, Sanskriti Chitransh, Shubham Chopda, Lavina Vedmutha, Sakshi Gore, Dhaval Gorhe, Akanksha Parakh, Karan Jadhav, Chaitali Bedmutha, Mehul Chopda, Gautami Kasat, Anand Nagapurkar, Ayush Shah and Shubham Bhadange, who were our sounding boards. Thank you for cheering us on throughout and allowing us to lean on you when the going got tough.

A special mention to Sahib Aggarwal, his parents and his sister Sehaj, who have been our ever-welcoming hosts in Delhi, and to Jai Sharma, for allowing us to crash at his place in Pune, making our trips to their cities to meet the interviewees possible.

To Gaurav's juniors at Dance Club and PEP, who provided unflinching help in refining the transcripts of the interviews. Thank you to Piyush Jain, Rahul Sunder, Mainak Mandal, Raghav Agrawal, Aparna M., Palvayi Revanth, Trinika Kaushik, Miloni Mittal, Joyotidisha Rajbongshi, Mitali Mehrotra, Anuj Maheshwari, Gandhar Kulkarni, Anirudh Parimi, Chaarvi Bansal, Anuneet Soni, Vratika Jain, Paarth Jain, Devansh Mishra, Bhaskar Rokana and Aastha Kataria.

To the amazing team at Pepper Content – Anirudh Singla, Rishabh Shekhar, Hemanshu Jain, Himanshu Goyal and Kishan Panpaliya – the unsung heroes who helped and inspired us in ways they don't know.

To Sachin Arya, head of Alumni & External Relations, and Professor Arya Kumar, Dean of Alumni Relations, for helping us institute a scholarship at BITS Pilani with the proceeds from our book to support the entrepreneurship culture at BITS Pilani.

To Ms Sandra (Mr Gulu Mirchandani's office), Ms Esha (Ms Tulsi Mirchandaney's office), Ms Mary (Mr Ajoy Misra's office), Mr Krishan (Mr Ajoy Bajoria's office), Ms Theresa and Ms Arlene (Mr Harish Bhat's office) and Ms Maria (Dr G. S. K. Velu's office) for coordinating with us and helping us with the interviews and reviews.

Special thanks to Mr Gajanan from Mr Prithviraj Chavan's office and Mr Phani Koundinya and Mr Yashwardhan Singh from Mr Baba Kalyani's office, who were very patient with our requests. Despite the busy schedules of Mr Chavan and Mr Kalyani, they helped us with the completion of our book.

Finally, our alma mater BITS Pilani, to which we will forever be indebted. In the four years we spent there, we found friends, mentors and well-wishers. The institution shaped us in innumerable ways and prodded us to become the best versions of ourselves. Our years there had the most profound impact on our personalities, and a large part of who we are and how we think today is owed to the conversations we had in college and the people we met on campus.